Awakening the Real You

Awakening the Real You

Awareness Through Dreams and Intuition

By
Nancy C. Pohle
and
Ellen L. Selover

ARE
PRESS

ASSOCIATION FOR
RESEARCH AND
ENLIGHTENMENT

A.R.E. Press • Virginia Beach • Virginia

A.R.E. Press
215 67th Street
Virginia Beach, VA 23451-2061

Library of Congress Cataloging-in-Publication Data
Pohle, Nancy C., 1950-
   Awakening the real you : awareness through dreams and intuition / Nancy C. Pohle and Ellen L. Selover.
      p.   cm.
   ISBN 0-87604-419-4
   1. Dreams. 2. Dream interpretation. 3. Intuition. 4. Cayce, Edgar, 1877-1945. Edgar Cayce readings. I. Selover, Ellen L., 1957- . II. Title.
BF1091.P64   1999
135'.3—dc21   98-43103

Cover design by Lightbourne Images

Dedications

I dedicate this book to my mother, Helen, and my late father, Stephen Kobrin, for so generously sharing their love, dreams, and intuitive genes with me.—Nancy

I dedicate this book to my parents, Lila and Will Selover, whose practical application of the spiritual principles in the Edgar Cayce readings provided safe harbor for the spiritual journeys of all their children.—Ellen

"If you bring forth what is within you,
what you bring forth will save you.
If you do not bring forth what is within you,
what you do not bring forth will destroy you."

Attributed to Jesus; from the introduction to
The Gnostic Gospels by Elaine Pagels

Contents

Acknowledgments

This book would not have been possible without the help of all the individuals and professionals who graciously contributed their stories, dreams, experiences, and expertise. Thanks to each of you for your willingness to share with us so openly in this endeavor.

We would like to thank Joseph Dunn for his support and encouragement, John Van Auken for first offering a book contract from A.R.E. Press, and Mark Thurston for endorsing this book for an A.R.E. membership benefit. Thanks are due also to our editors Jon Robertson, Lynda Kenny, and Ken Skidmore, and to Kathleen Sparrow for her helpful input during the initial planning.

From Nancy: I am deeply grateful to my family, especially to my sister, Pat, and brother, Steve, for years of discussing their dreams at the breakfast table; to John Pohle for suggesting years ago that I write a book about my and others' dream experiences; to my daughters Jessica and Rachel for all their love and intuitive insights; and to my granddaughter, Caroline Elizabeth, who warms my heart and served as an inspiration to complete the book. My gratitude extends to Susan and Una for their wonderful friendship. My sincerest thanks also go to Dennis Chrisbaum for his unflagging moral support, humor, and loving but incisive suggestions throughout this project.

Immeasurable gratitude is due to Edgar Cayce for having the courage to share what he knew to be true about the nature of the soul.

Finally, and, most importantly, I am ever grateful to the Christ Spirit which guides us all to creatively express the highest within us.

From Ellen: My deepest appreciation and thanks go to Denise Furgason, for her steadfast support, optimism, and encouragement; to friends Anne, Bob, Kevin, Mary,

Meredith, and Pete for helping me to dream the dream; and to my entire family who, though we each see the world through a different lens, shared with me their own visions and offered support, suggestions, and a few stories of their own.

PREFACE

IT ISN'T EASY BEING alive in the world today. But we each have chosen to be here at this time for very specific reasons unique to ourselves. Ultimately, those reasons merge, leading us back to the one great Source from which we all came.

Our journeys back to that all-knowing, all-loving Spirit can be whatever we make them. They can be glorious adventures into new realms of awareness and understanding, or they can just as easily be arduous treks, fraught with anxiety and self-imposed limitations. The choice is ours. We each have been gifted with a spark of divine energy that bears our own special mark. Once that spark is ignited, its currents send an electrical charge to other tiny sparks, eventually creating a magnificent flame of extraordinary beauty and power. The force of that combined energy becomes a flame so intense in its warmth and strength that it once again merges with the one great Divine Source.

We have the needed insight and awareness within us to find our way back. But which way will we choose? If we accept the gifts of awareness that have been given to us through our dreams and intuitive perceptions, the pathway becomes more clear.

Many of the principles outlined in this book come from the work of Edgar Cayce, known throughout the world for his psychic discourses. Cayce was a humble man whose greatest wish in life was to be of help to people. Early in his youth he displayed remarkable abilities, including sleeping on his school books to remember, verbatim, the information in his lessons; seeing and conversing with his deceased grandfather; and playing with "spirit" children. While in his early twenties, he discovered an ability to put himself into a hypnotic sleep and, with his unconscious mind, to actually see into his own body, provide a physical diagnosis for a debilitating laryngitis, and suggest treatments for the ultimate healing of that condition.

He soon found that he could use this ability to help others in much the same way and over the course of many years provided such psychic "readings" for thousands of people. Eventually, people requesting readings began to ask questions of a more esoteric nature— questions regarding the nature of humankind and the purpose of life; the attributes of dreams and the unconscious mind; the relationship of body, mind, and spirit; psychic phenomena and creativity. Thousands of topics were addressed in this material, which was transcribed verbatim.

Though Edgar Cayce passed away in 1945, his legacy lives on through the readings, which are available today for personal study through the Association for Research and Enlightenment, Inc., in Virginia Beach, Virginia. The quotes we have chosen that begin each chapter and that are interspersed throughout the book are taken from his readings, which were numbered for indexing purposes and to maintain the anonymity of the recipient.

The ideas presented in this book are intended to remind us of all those special qualities waiting to be reignited with the flame of our higher purpose. We sincerely hope that you will find these suggestions beneficial during your personal journey home. In the words of the Edgar Cayce readings, "The only real life [is] that which in the material or physical plane is called psychic . . . Ridicule of such forces . . . " is to be "pitied" rather than "condemned." (3744-2)

1

AWAKENING THE REAL YOU

What then is the purpose of the entity's activity in the consciousness of mind, matter, spirit in the present? That it, the entity, may *know* itself to *be* itself and . . . one *with* the whole . . . 826-11

IT CAN BE INTRIGUING and pleasantly distracting to speculate on why we have been born at this time. Maybe we find it comforting to think of ourselves as being special, even *chosen*, to be alive at this purported era of destiny. Although it's true that we *are* special and have certainly been given a great opportunity to be alive at this pivotal time, we need to find the wherewithal to admit and accept a very important fact: In spite of our uniqueness as individuals, we are still only tiny cogs in a magnificent and complex cosmic wheel. Can we accept this truth and still discern the grandeur that is divinely woven throughout our daily lives? "Surely, there must be more," we might say to ourselves, or, to borrow a lyric, "Is that all there is, my friend?"

Well, in one sense, yes, that *is* all that there is. On the other hand, how little we truly perceive of what our lives can be! Ideally, it seems most beneficial to strike a balance between the two ways of thinking. If we spend a great deal of our time looking beyond the present moment rather than appreciating what's going on in the here and now, it's easy to feel that life is, in some way, passing us by. We begin to erroneously believe that all the uplifting and interesting experiences are happening to someone else. Or, perhaps, we fantasize about trading places with a famous guru or well-known psychic whose life seems to transcend what we view as reality. If we limit ourselves by thinking that the potential for a rich and spiritually evolved life is only available to a chosen few, then we are doing ourselves a great disservice.

In fact, the Cayce readings and numerous philosophical texts portray a very different picture. They tell us that we all come from one great Source where infinite energy and limitless potential abound. They also explain that within the One Force we are each an individual soul with very special gifts and that part of our purpose for being alive is to express those gifts. That expression, by its very nature, is a lifelong process.

One way to describe this process is to say that we each have a different way of connecting with our Creator, and the manner in which we connect could be considered as our own intuitive network or lifeline to the Higher Source. The possibility of making that connection is always present, always available. But, for numerous reasons, we frequently choose *not* to take advantage of the energy, wisdom, and tremendous comfort that are available to us. It's as if we have paid the cable company to hook us up for all options offered, but we never turn on the television.

So how do we go about turning on the TV and fine-tuning our reception in order to understand and utilize this tremendous capacity? It is crucial first to have a good understanding of ourselves and the nature of humanity. We must discover why we are here and how we can best fulfill our own soul's purpose.

If we operate from the above premise—that we all come from the same One Force—then we can understand the concept that we are each children of God, the Creator. Because God is Spirit, we, as creations of that Spirit, are also spiritual beings. When we were first created, we had an awareness of and access to all the wisdom and divine energy of the Infinite. When we came into material existence in the earth plane, we shifted our awareness away from the Divine Infinite and focused it into the conscious, finite realm. A drifting apart took place, making it difficult to have direct access to or even to remember our birthright as spiritual beings.

Our present level of awareness exists within the three-dimensional world, manifesting as the conscious, subconscious, and superconscious. These correspond directly to what we might call the three aspects of ourselves: the physical body, the mental body, and the spiritual body. Our soul is the spiritual body, encompassing the vital energies of spirit, mind, and free will.

Perhaps one of the most essential keys to understanding our divine nature is to recognize the tremendous power available to us through the application of our own mental attitude and free will. Every choice we make, whether it is choosing to incarnate into the earth or deciding where to go on vacation, is an expression of that will. The Cayce readings tell us that one of the greatest lessons we can learn in the earth plane is to align our own will with that of God's. We do this by remembering our divine nature and consciously choosing to express unconditional love in our relationships with others, with ourselves, and even with God. Over time, that expression brings about the attunement of our small self with the greater collective God self. That is, in effect, our greatest purpose: to comprehend how to make our way back to the Godhead.

Although our direct connection with the Godhead and with our own divine nature is somewhat obscure to us in our everyday lives, the Cayce readings assure us that there are avenues through which we can gain conscious insight into and information from this core aspect of our beings. One of these is intuition, described by the Edgar Cayce readings as "the innate cry for expression of the inner self." (531-1) Another avenue is dream exploration, on which Cayce offered this insight: " . . . there is not sufficient credence given dreams; for the best development of the human family is to give the greater increase in knowledge of the subconscious, soul or spirit world. This is a *dream.*" (3744-5) The process of learning to recognize, correctly interpret, and respond to the information we receive through intuition and dreams *is* the process of remembering our divine nature and aligning our will to that of the Divine.

With those ideas in mind, it is essential that we take steps that will enhance our ability to attune to the Creator. As we make that attunement, the information we receive through our dreams and intuition becomes clearer and stronger, providing vital information and feedback for us in our spiritual development. Meditation, prayer, and working with ideals are the most effective tools we can use to plant our feet firmly on the path of spiritual development and, thereby, strengthen our connection with the Creator.

Meditation and Prayer

It is interesting to note that the combined use of meditation and prayer was recommended repeatedly in the Cayce material, not only for spiritual growth, but also for physical, mental, and emotional healing. Most world religions incorporate prayer, but not all suggest the use of meditation, at least not in the comprehensive, regularly applied way we are suggesting here. We believe that these disciplines are actually prerequisites to intuitive development, since our personal experience has confirmed the readings' assertion that intuitive/psychic abilities actually come about as a byproduct of soul growth. So, as we progress spiritually in our attunement with the Creative Forces, we can expect our psychic perceptions to increase and improve as a result.

There are a number of excellent books that give extensive explanations of both meditation and prayer, and we have listed some of these in the reading list at the end of the book. For a preliminary understanding of these practices, however, let's reflect on the definitions of these terms in the Cayce readings. We'll begin with meditation.

What *is* Meditation?

It is not musing, not daydreaming; but as ye find your bodies made up of the physical, mental and spiritual, it is the attuning of the mental body and the physical body to its spiritual source.

. . . it is the attuning of thy physical and mental attributes seeking to know the relationships to the Maker. *That* is true meditation. 281-41

. . . Meditation, then, is prayer, but is prayer from *within* the *inner* self, and partakes not only of the physical inner [person] but the soul that is aroused by the spirit of [the person] from within. 281-13

. . . for ye are *raising* in meditation actual *creation* taking place within the inner self! 281-13

As we begin to incorporate meditation into our daily routine, we also begin to create a more spiritual lifestyle. This is so because, by taking the time consistently to attune our individual wills to the Higher Will of the Creator, we automatically start to heighten our awareness and become mindful of the daily choices we make in our lives. Each activity we perform on a physical or mental level affects what occurs during meditation, and vice versa.

For example, if an individual spends a lot of time watching horror movies on TV and eats unhealthy food while doing so, this will have a direct impact on the quality of that person's meditation. The body will have difficulty digesting the food, which in turn will create distracting physical conditions that will adversely affect the person's ability to relax, breathe, and remain still during meditation. Additionally, a mental "diet" of horror movies can evoke a residue of troubling images that lurk in that person's consciousness for a time, making it difficult to focus on the uplifting quality of the affirmation during meditation. Therefore, anything we can do to create optimum conditions in our physical and mental bodies will have a positive influence on our ability to achieve spiritual attunement.

Simply put, prayer is talking to God, and meditation is listening. Recognizing how the two practices complement one another is an essential ingredient to developing a well-balanced approach to spiritual development. In her book, *Healing Through Meditation and Prayer,* Meredith Puryear states that "We pray in order to meditate and meditate in order to pray most effectively." It was recommended in the Cayce readings that we always begin each meditation session with prayer, both for protection and attunement, and end each meditation by praying for others.

. . . prayer is the *making* of one's conscious self more in attune with the spiritual forces that may manifest in a material world . . . Prayer is the concerted effort of the physical consciousness to become attuned to the consciousness of the Creator, either collectively or individually. 281-13

. . . remember the injunction—never worry as long as you can pray. When you can't pray—you'd better begin to worry! For then you have something to worry about! 3569-1

A Meditation Procedure from the Edgar Cayce Readings

1. Set aside a daily time period for your meditation. Regularity helps you to remember to meditate, and, as you keep the time each day, it becomes easier to get your mind quiet and focused. Choose a time when you are most awake, least distracted, and most able to keep focused on your spiritual life and ideals. When you are first beginning to meditate, keep your session brief, perhaps just a few minutes. As you become more practiced, you may feel the desire to increase the time.
2. Create an environment which will best assist you in getting quiet and focused on your spiritual life. Here are some ways of aiding your attunement. As you work with them, you will find those with which you resonate.
   a) Read an inspirational passage from the Bible or other spiritual literature.
   b) Focus on your breathing.
   c) Stretch your head and neck (forward and backward, from side to side, and in circles in both directions).
   d) Chant.

e) Burn incense.
f) Listen to inspirational, sacred, or quieting, centering music.
3. Take a few moments for prayer to ask for spiritual protection and to attune your mind in preparation for entering the stillness. Many people use prayers from their religious traditions, such as the Lord's Prayer, while others find that a spontaneous expression from the heart is helpful.
4. Use an affirmation to bring your mind and your attention to a point of spiritual focus. This affirmation can be as simple or complex as you need. One example is *"Be still, and know that I am God."* (Other examples of affirmations taken from the *Search for God* books are included in the appendix.)
5. Repeat your affirmation several times, aloud if you wish, then move to a silent, gentle repetition in your mind. True meditation begins when you start to feel the meaning of the words, to sense the spirit which the words represent. When you begin to feel this inner meaning, silently focus on this spirit, this feeling. If you feel your attention drift, simply guide it back by repeating the affirmation and holding that feeling in silence.
6. At the end of this period of silence, take time again for prayer, focusing on prayer for others. If there are people who have specifically asked for your prayers in healing or for changing a situation, then it is fine to pray specifically for that. Otherwise, pray for people for whom you have concern by blessing them and asking that they be surrounded in the pure white light.

The Seven Spiritual Centers

When we enter into meditation to attune our physical bodies, what we are actually doing is seeking to bring balance and wholeness to two separate but intricately entwined energy systems, the etheric body and the physical body. In the etheric body are seven spiritual centers, known as *chakras*, the Sanskrit word for *wheels*. The chakras exist in what Edgar Cayce called the "finer physical body," which is a complete replica of the physical body in energy form. Many Eastern and Western esoteric traditions teach the existence of these centers. They have been depicted in religious texts and artwork for centuries as halos and other light emanations.

One way to think about these centers is to imagine them as swirling vortices of light energy. They serve as points of contact between our physical bodies and the soul through which subtle energy flows. This energy flows in two ways: from the spirit into the body, and from one spiritual center to another. The chakras also serve to store memory patterns of the soul.

Each center has a particular purpose (see figure, p. 11). The first four centers, known as the lower chakras, symbolize our manifestation as physical beings in a material world. The first center, or root chakra, is located at the base of the spine and brings to the body the basic survival, self-preservation energies. The second chakra is located in the lower abdomen and relates to the balance between the masculine and feminine energies which are in each of us. The third center is in the solar plexus and relates to the use of personal power in the material world. When that center is balanced, we experience the positive use of that power through courage and initiative. When that center is out of balance, we might experience anger, resentment, or fear. The fourth center is known as the heart chakra. It is the center of love at the personal, human level. In its most balanced state, we might experience compassion, love, and openness. When it is out of balance, envy, jealousy, or worry may cloud our emotional landscape. The next three spiritual centers are known as the higher chakras, representing the divine aspects within us all. The fifth center, located at the throat, is the seat of free will. When it is in balance, we can express our will by making independent decisions that are in accord with and responsive to God's will. When it is out of balance, we might experience willfulness or indecisiveness. The sixth center, known as the brow or third eye chakra, is located behind the forehead and is related to the higher mind, the universal Christ Consciousness, intuition, and imagination. The seventh center, or crown chakra, is at the top of the head and represents oneness, divine wisdom, and spiritual healing. These centers are our contact with the Divine.

Each chakra also relates to specific endocrine glands within the body, creating the link among the body, the mind, and the spirit. These glands secrete hormones into the blood, controlling a multitude of physiological responses. Physical health and disease are influenced by the operation of the endocrine system, which is, in turn, influenced by the spiritual centers. When we seek to balance the spiritual centers through various tools of attunement, we can also balance and purify the physical body through the endocrine system.

Edgar Cayce suggested that when Jesus taught His disciples to pray the Lord's Prayer, He was giving them a tool with which to balance both the physical centers, that is, the endocrine glands and the chakras.

In his book, *Creative Meditation*, Richard Peterson describes this relationship: "Key words within that prayer speak directly to the seven centers; for example, 'heaven' refers to the pituitary and 'name' to the pineal— both in the head; 'will' refers to the thyroid in the throat;

THE LORD'S PRAYER
AND THE SEVEN CENTERS

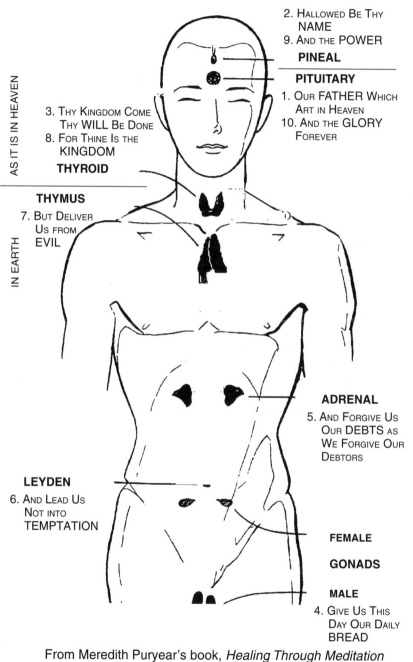

2. HALLOWED BE THY NAME
9. AND THE POWER
PINEAL

PITUITARY
1. OUR FATHER WHICH ART IN HEAVEN
10. AND THE GLORY FOREVER

AS IT IS IN HEAVEN

3. THY KINGDOM COME THY WILL BE DONE
8. FOR THINE IS THE KINGDOM
THYROID

THYMUS
7. BUT DELIVER US FROM EVIL

IN EARTH

ADRENAL
5. AND FORGIVE US OUR DEBTS AS WE FORGIVE OUR DEBTORS

LEYDEN
6. AND LEAD US NOT INTO TEMPTATION

FEMALE

GONADS

MALE
4. GIVE US THIS DAY OUR DAILY BREAD

From Meredith Puryear's book, *Healing Through Meditation and Prayer,* A.R.E. Press, 1978.

'deliverance from evil' refers to the thymus near the heart: 'forgiveness of debts' to the adrenals in the solar plexus; 'freedom from temptation' to the cells of Leydig in the gonads; and 'daily bread' to the gonads themselves." In addition, the phrase "in earth" relates to the four lower centers, while "as it is in heaven" refers to the three higher centers.

Ideals

If we recognize just how important our free will is in determining the outcome of our life experiences, we will also understand the necessity of setting the very highest standards possible for the choices we make. That is precisely what an ideal does for us. It gives us a frame of reference within which to measure our decisions, even those seemingly insignificant ones that present themselves to us moment by moment.

There is a simple procedure we can follow in order to set ideals for ourselves, with specific steps taken directly from material presented in the Edgar Cayce readings. The following quote sums up very succinctly just how essential Cayce's source believed the setting of an ideal to be in each person's spiritual and intuitive development: " . . . the most important experience of this or any individual entity is to first know what *is* the ideal—spiritually." (357-13)

Before setting an ideal, it is important to differentiate between an ideal and a goal. A goal is something tangible, desired, and attainable, whereas an ideal could be defined as the motivational standard used to measure our methods and/or reasons for pursuing a particular goal. An ideal allows us to evaluate our true purpose for choosing an activity and lets us determine whether we feel good about the action being taken. In other words, are we performing our daily activities in a spirit that meets our highest standards, or are we simply taking the easy way out and doing whatever fulfills our self-oriented desires at a given moment? What feels good is not necessarily the wrong choice, nor do our decisions always have to be unpleasant or painful. However, we need to develop discernment in recognizing our own purposes and motives as we progress on our spiritual path.

Another definition for an ideal is an *incentive* or *pattern that guides our lives.* This is particularly significant when we understand that, from the readings' viewpoint, we are all working with ideals on a subconscious level, whether we realize it or not. Even at those times when we choose not to make a decision about something, we are still making a choice. By not honing in on a point of focus in our lives, we allow outside circumstances to decide for us, thereby passively accepting an outcome that may either spur or deter growth.

Here's an analogy. If you were planning to visit a friend's home for the first time, it's unlikely that you would hop in your car and randomly try to find the address. It's much more sensible to ask for specific details, thereby increasing the probability that you would actually arrive at the home. It's really no different than the process of setting a spiritual ideal for our lives. An ideal serves as a "spiritual road map" to guide us to our ultimate destination of awareness of the Divine within.

Working with ideals allows us to consciously assess our thoughts, emotions, and actions in our daily lives, in our interpersonal relationships, and in our relationship with God. Cayce suggested that one method for doing this is to take a piece of paper and on it draw three columns. In the first column, write the word "spiritual"; in the second column, write "mental"; and in the third, write "physical."

Then, through prayer and meditation, allow yourself

to become clear about the most sublime purpose you can imagine, and formulate that into a spiritual ideal. This ideal is one that makes your heart joyous, that speaks to your soul. Cayce said, " . . . thy spiritual concept of the ideal, whether it be Jesus, Buddha, mind, material, God or whatever is the word which indicates to self the ideals spiritual." (5091-3) An example of this type of ideal might be "unconditional love" or "oneness." A spiritual ideal is usually a word or succinct phrase. Write that ideal in the first column.

The next step is to consider positive mental or emotional attributes that would help you reach your spiritual ideal through conscious choices about the attitudes you hold, the thoughts you think, or the emotions you feel and express. Such ideals might be expressed as "patience with self and others" or "being nonjudgmental." The readings define this as " . . . the ideal mental attitude, as may arise from concepts of the spiritual, in relationship to self, to home, to friends, to neighbors, to thy enemies, to things, to conditions." (5091-3) There can be several mental ideals. Write these down in the second column.

Finally, consider those conditions in the environment or physical activities that would help to support the strengthening of your mental and spiritual ideals. Examples of physical ideals might be "treating my body as a temple of God through proper diet and exercise" or "daily prayer and meditation." Write these physical ideals in the third column.

Here is what our simple ideals chart looks like. As you begin to work with your own chart, include in the mental and physical ideals columns as many items as you feel are necessary to help you direct your intent and actions toward manifesting your spiritual ideal.

Sample Ideals Chart

Spiritual Ideal	Mental Ideals	Physical Ideals
Unconditional Love	Patience with self and others	Daily prayer and meditation
	Being nonjudgmental	Treating my body as a temple of God through proper diet and exercise

The Cayce readings suggest that we review and rework our ideals charts on a regular basis to help us keep them in mind and to fine-tune them as we progress along our spiritual journey. And of course, writing them down is just a first step; application of those ideals in our day-to-day lives is the key.

Then set about to apply the knowledge ye have attained, for ye will get ideas and that ideal. Ye may change them from period to period, as ye study them over. For as ye apply them they become thy ideals. To be just as theories they do not belong to thee, they are still theories so far as thy personal being is concerned. It's the application of same that counts. What do they bring into thine experience? These are well if ye will apply them. 5091-3

A True-Life Example

Sometimes choosing an ideal in life is really just becoming conscious about what we are already doing in our lives to express the highest within. In the following, our friend Midge shares her experience with learning to recognize her ideals. Notice that when she chose to become a mother, she recognized the importance of choosing to live each day with the intent of being the best parent that she could. This brought her joy and fulfillment, even though she did not consciously label either of these as her ideal. Later in life, when she asked herself the question, What is it that makes my heart sing? she recalled that her experiences in raising children and teaching a parenting class were ones during which she felt closely connected with her higher self. As Midge reaffirms that ideal, dreams and synchronistic events seemed to support her in her discovery.

"Many years ago, when I was sixteen, I had a child whom I had to give up for adoption. This experience of giving birth and then losing that child gave me a tremendous appreciation for the experience of parenting. When I finally had children whom I could keep, it meant a great deal to me that I parent them the best I could. I wanted very much to instill in them a sense of themselves, to teach them to take responsibility for their actions, and, most importantly, I wanted to be sure that they knew they were loved.

"I spent many years just concentrating on being their mother. I made many mistakes along the way, but I learned a great deal. In 1993, when I came to Virginia, I wanted to do some community service and became involved in teaching a parenting class. Many of my students had been mandated by the courts to attend my class because their children had been removed from the home due to physical or sexual abuse. Outside of raising Ian and Lacy, it was the most fulfilling work I had ever done.

"Four years later, I read the chapter on ideals in Henry Reed's book *Your Mind* and realized how very important it is to set an ideal for my life. So, naturally, I proceeded to follow the steps that help define the ideal. One of these steps entailed identifying things in life which made me feel joy and fulfillment. I identified those occasions in my life as raising my kids and teaching that parenting class. So, of course, I realized that I have to find something similar to do in order to live my ideal."

Midge asked for a dream to clarify her ideals that night. The next morning, all she could remember about her dream was that it involved her parents and the director of youth services where she worked. After Midge discussed this dream and related thoughts about the true nature of parenting with a co-worker, the co-worker suggested that she contact the director of youth services about teaching a parenting course. Within a few minutes, that very person knocked on her office door to chat about another matter. Instantly, Midge recognized that this was the clarity for which she was looking, and she made a commitment to teach the parenting class.

Other Avenues of Spiritual Attunement

Food for the soul. Just as our physical bodies need healthful foods and a balance of activity, our spiritual selves thrive on positive, affirmative input. Spiritually uplifting music or reading material can be extremely beneficial. Anything that is personally enriching is appropriate (for example, the music of Hildegard of Bingen or Gregorian chants, the poetry of Kahlil Gibran and other authors, sacred texts such as the Bible and Koran, or devotional material such as Unity Church's *Daily Word*, A.R.E.'s *Think on These Things,* or *Meditations of Paramahansa Yogananda*). Edgar Cayce particularly recommended reading Deuteronomy 30 in the Old Testament and John 14 through 17 in the New Testament of the Bible, for anyone studying the nature of intuition.

Develop a support network with others on a spiritual path. In these fast-paced times, it is sometimes difficult to maintain focus on our spiritual journeys in practical ways. A support group can help us in this endeavor. By connecting with others of like mind, studying and discussing spiritual ideas, and making a commitment to support one another, group members create a community in which personal and spiritual growth are the priority. The A.R.E.'s Search for God program is one example of an excellent spiritual support group.

Inspirational writing. The Cayce readings suggest that when we are in a quiet, spiritually focused state of mind, we can open ourselves to creative insights and inspiration that come directly from our higher selves. Not to be confused with automatic writing, which is opening one's self to channel information from another entity, inspirational writing is a practice of communicating with one's own source. Once an attunement is made, as after meditation, simply take paper and pen and begin to write whatever comes to mind. Asking a specific question helps to focus the intent for guidance.

Conclusion

The process of understanding who we are as spiritual beings in a three-dimensional world is a complex one. The suggestions in this chapter are intended to provide effective tools to bring that understanding into our conscious awareness and into our everyday experience in very practical ways. When we pay conscious attention to that journey, we become active participants in our spiritual growth. The natural outgrowth of this participation is increased awareness of ourselves, our environment, and our relationships to God and to one another.

2

INTUITIVE AWARENESS

The more and more each is impelled by that which is intuitive, or the relying upon the soul force within, the greater, the farther, the deeper, the broader, the more constructive may be the result . . . 792-2

INFORMATION IS ALL AROUND us. By merely turning on the radio, tuning in to a television channel, or clicking onto the Internet, we can have instant access to an incomprehensible amount of data. The key to sending and receiving this information is the intricate network of transmitters and receivers around the globe. We would be astounded if we could see all the sound waves, laser beams, impulses, and signals that cross back and forth beyond our levels of perception.

Our bodies are also powerful transmitters and receivers. We transmit through our voice and inflection, choices of words, facial expressions, actions, and body language. Likewise, our physical senses—hearing, sight, taste, smell, and touch—are powerful receptors, able to retrieve immense amounts of information every second. They send signals through the nervous system to the brain, which then processes and responds to that information with messages and impulses.

A simple way to become aware of these processes is to think about the information we receive upon stepping outdoors. Our senses instantly perceive and relay to the brain signals regarding the change in temperature, the moisture content in the air, the intensity of the sun, the flight of a bird, or the whine of a nearby lawnmower. We might smell the pungent odor of grease and oil or the unmistakable aroma of a backyard barbecue. All of these elements provide us with instant information about this new environment.

On the mental level, we transmit information through every thought we think and each emotion we express. These go out from us in the form of energy which can be perceived by others. Though we may often be unaware of the source of the signal, we still may pick up on the finer vibrations of thought and emotion, just as we do the physical sensations. We transmit and receive this information in a similar pattern, even though the energies are difficult to measure.

Mirka Knaster, author of *Discovering the Body's Wisdom*, suggests that the body's internal network of sensory receptors provides us with proprioception (awareness of the precise position of our body) and kinesthesia (the awareness of direction of movement) which, combined, function as a sixth sense, allowing us to know where we are in space and time. According to Knaster, it is these proprioceptors which pick up energy emanating from other people and other creatures around us.

On yet another energy level—the spiritual—we become aware of influences and information through intuition. When we lay the groundwork for a spiritual connection to one another and to God, we sharpen these higher senses of receptivity. Intuition is our greatest link to our higher selves (our spiritual selves) and thus to God.

> . . . Seek not from without, but to those consciousnesses, those voices, those feelings, those vibrations as may arise from within. For know, as has been indicated, *there* He, the Giver of all good and perfect gifts, makes to grow those seeds which ye have sown. 1991-1

The regular practice of meditation allows us to tune in to our higher senses and clear our sensory systems of the *static* of other influences. We become cognizant of the impulses that arise from within with which we truly resonate. Everything we do to become more spiritually attuned improves our ability to understand, interpret, and follow through on the guidance we receive.

One way to understand how this process works is to imagine a playground full of excited children, with a parent sitting on a sideline. That parent is so well attuned, so familiar with his or her own child's voice, that he or she can, at any given moment, instantly pick out that voice from all the others on the playground. So it is with intuition. As we become more spiritually attuned, we can better pinpoint the "sound" of our higher self, or of God, and learn to recognize it.

Forms of Guidance:
How People Actually Experience Intuition

The intuitive impressions we receive come to us in a variety of different ways. As you read the following descriptions and examples, we hope that you catch a glimpse of the intriguing and often unanticipated ways that intuitive impressions can be experienced. Perhaps you will recognize your own talents below and realize that you are psychic after all!

Clairvoyance (clear seeing or clear vision) is experienced when an individual discerns objects, people, or situations, not with the physical eyes, but with an internal sense sometimes referred to as the "third eye." Such "visions" concern something beyond one's physical view, e.g., in the next room, down the street, or a thousand miles away.

On several occasions, Edgar Cayce exhibited clairvoyance during a reading. While at his home in Virginia Beach, Cayce could describe what the person was wearing at the time of a reading or comment on the scenery around the person's home, even if the individual was hundreds of miles away. Another example of his clairvoyance became apparent while playing card games. He could literally see the faces of the cards that his opponents were holding. Because of this, he refused to play card games due to his unfair advantage.

Clairaudience (clear hearing) is the ability to receive thoughts or information about a person or situation through an auditory sense instead of a visual one. This information is actually inaudible to the normal hearing range. It can be experienced as delicate sounds such as music, bells, or singing. It might also manifest as a knocking, siren, or other attention-getting sound. Most often, it comes as a voice that is literally heard either directly in the brain or through the auditory sense, as if it comes from beside or behind the person.

This voice can have many aspects, at times sounding like the person's own, and at others taking on a change of tone, volume, or pitch and sounding like someone else. It can take on an authoritarian tone or that of warning, gentle prodding, or encouragement. It can also be very objective and matter-of-fact.

Lila shared her experience of learning to work with this type of intuition: "I learned as a child that if I wanted to just try to discover something, I could look at some plant or a tree, and kind of go within. And I found that when I asked a specific question and listened—there's a very deep listening involved—I could get answers that way, and many of them were the kind that would be comforting."

Through Lila's focused development of this faculty, she was eventually able to receive information for others. This information came in response to a friend's need. Roslyn and Sol were expecting their third child. When she received the call that Ros had given birth to a little girl, Lila was overjoyed. With their two boys, the family was now complete.

Lila went shopping for a greeting card to send to Ros and Sol. As she reached for a card, a shocking impression came: "*Ros and Sol are very worried about their baby, but she will be all right.*" Deeply concerned, Lila purchased the card and went home, thinking, "If anything was wrong, Ros would have told me!"

Though she doubted the accuracy of the message, Lila did pass it along in a note to Ros, who later called her. In a voice filled with heartbreak, Ros explained that her daughter had been born with a severe cleft palate. She and Sol were devastated, and Lila's note had been their first ray of hope. The intuitive message proved to be correct over time. After many operations, the child's condition was corrected, and she grew up to be a beautiful woman.

Clairsentience (clear sensing) is probably the most frequent way intuition manifests in our lives, through hunches, gut feelings, or a sense of knowing without knowing how one knows. This "sensing" is often accompanied by a physical sensation—for some people in the solar plexus, for others in the heart area. Some feel a prickling of their skin. The physical sensation can vary with each person.

This information comes to us in a variety of ways. At times, it comes as a thought that walks across the mind in a natural, subtle manner. When intuition comes to us in this way, it is so much like the regular musings of our mind that we can easily miss it, dismiss it, or mistake it for our own ruminations.

This "knowing" can also come to us in the form of advice on one's personal life. Author and lecturer Rob Grant recounted the intuition he received regarding his move to Virginia Beach to work at the Association for Research and Enlightenment.

"I had gotten out of the navy and had gone back home to Indiana. I had been in broadcasting—the newspaper business and TV—and so my dad thought that was what I would pursue. I was signed up for college . . . then I got the copy of A.R.E.'s *Venture Inward* magazine that talked about computerizing the [Edgar Cayce] readings. Ever since I was sixteen, I had been interested in the readings. When I saw that article, I didn't just think, 'Oh, I'd like to do that.' Instead, I knew without a doubt, '*I am going to Virginia Beach to do this.*' It seemed startling, because it wasn't a thought, but a knowing. In retrospect, I see it was the clear voice of the Divine speaking through my intuition. At the same time, I thought I was a little crazy, because it dawned on me, 'I'm not going to college?!'

"The most difficult part was trying to convey to my friends and loved ones why I had made this choice, when outwardly it just didn't make any sense. I was going to move to Virginia Beach, and I knew I would be part of this project. And so it was simultaneously an unsettling but euphoric feeling. There was no mistake that it wasn't just a thought, and it wasn't just wishful thinking. My father said, 'So, you're going to Virginia Beach to pursue a job you don't have yet, right?' The hardest thing about it was my family and friends thinking I was a little crazy.

"But I drove to Virginia Beach, and all the while felt a sense of trepidation, but it never stopped me. As a result of that move, I was able to do this amazing work with the readings, which led to my work as a writer and speaker. So the people who once questioned my judgment now say, 'my son, the author' or 'my friend, the author.' As I look back, I see now why that came through so clearly. It was the result of my asking, 'What am I supposed to do?' It was really like a prayer."

In following his intuition to move to Virginia Beach, Rob made a decision which proved to be life-changing. Had he followed his plan to attend college, it might have been a *good*, sensible decision. However, his choice to follow the wisdom of his inner promptings resulted in a life path he might never have imagined otherwise.

Yet another way this "knowing" manifests is through what Edgar Cayce described as the "high sensitive feelings." (421-5) We might experience concern for a friend, a feeling of dread that our child is in need, nervousness in the presence of unknown danger, or even profound joy at the awareness of God's love. This type of intuition can also be experienced as a vague sense of discomfort that is hard to define, and even harder to dispel. Marilyn shared such an experience.

"Once at summer camp when I was young, I was in my cabin with my bunkmates at rest period. We were playing cards and carrying on until my counselor asked us to quiet down and to go rest in our respective bunks. I had the top bunk opposite my counselor, who was also in an upper bunk. After a few minutes of reading, I started to feel very unsettled, like something was going to happen, but I didn't know what. I prayed silently and asked what, if anything, I should do. Immediately after the prayer, the thought came into my mind that I should get down out of my bunk. When I did so, I felt foolish just standing in the middle of the floor, so I began to pick up the cards that we had strewn about the cabin. The feeling of anxiety left immediately and was forgotten. Everyone else was asleep by then, so I tiptoed quietly so as not to disturb them. There were a few cards on the empty bunk below my counselor's bed. Just as I bent over to gather them, she stirred and rolled over the edge of her bed, landing squarely on my back. She had been sound asleep, but awoke suddenly upon impact, and was completely disoriented. I was shocked and embarrassed, and had to crawl out from under her. Although she suffered a broken collar bone, we realized that if someone or something had not been there to break her fall, she might have hit her head on the hard suitcase that was lying on the floor by her bunk and might have suffered an even greater injury."

Although Marilyn did not understand the source of her uneasiness, her desire to be of assistance and her attunement through prayer put her in the right place at the right time. The desire to be of service can be a clarifying force, guiding your actions even if you do not know why.

Intuition Through the Other Senses

We can also experience intuition through our senses of taste and smell, known as clairsavorance and clairscent, respectively, though these are not as common as the others. In one reading (5163-1), a woman asked Cayce what was the meaning of a particular scent that she smelled in the house periodically. His response was that it was the intuition that she needed to cultivate—not an omen, but an influence that would be ever present. Some people have reported the experience of smelling a particular scent, such as lilacs or warm chocolate chip cookies, that they associated with a special person at the moment when that person passed away. It is also reported that people frequently smell the scent of roses whenever apparitions of Mother Mary occur.

The Perception of Vibration

Intuition can also manifest as the discernment of energy or vibration, which can take many forms.

Telepathy is thought transference from the subconscious of one individual to that of another. This takes place nonverbally and is commonly referred to as "mind reading."

The following story was conveyed to us by Lee, a mother who encountered an unmistakable case of telepathic communication with her two-year-old daughter many years ago.

"I was in the process of organizing my day's activities to make room for an evening out with my husband. I decided that I should give Erin a bath right away rather than later at night when we returned. I no sooner thought those words than my two year old looked up at me with pleading eyes and said quite adamantly, 'But, Mommy, I don't want to take a bath right now.' After the initial shock at her response to my nonverbal idea, I suddenly realized just how true the statement 'thoughts are things' really is!"

Aura Perception is the ability to see the energy field surrounding all living beings and inanimate objects as well. The Cayce readings refer to this field as an "emanation of the soul." The aura's colors and vibration can indicate the condition and health of one's physical body, the mental/emotional state of one's mind, and the level of one's spiritual development.

The ability to see auras is one that may come naturally, as with many young children, or can be developed over time. Our young friend Erin, who could so easily pick up on her mother's thoughts, also displayed the ability to perceive auras several years later when she was in kindergarten. She came home from school one day and began telling her mother about the "shadows" she saw around people. After a trip to the eye doctor, who said that Erin had perfect vision, Lee pursued the concept of "shadows" more fully in a conversation with her child.

Erin explained how she would usually see "pink shadows" around some of her friends at school. "Your shadow is blue most of the time, Mommy. And Daddy's is kind of yellow-gold, except when he's mad, 'cause then it turns red! But, when I get scared at night I come into your bedroom, because you and Dad glow in the dark like night lights."

Erin's ability to see auras did not seem unusual to her; she assumed that everyone saw colors around each other. Erin's mother observed that seeing the colors was less significant than the fact that her daughter's sensitivity to people's energy patterns and vibrations enhanced her capacity to be compassionate, diplomatic, and cognizant of others' needs.

Perception of other realms. Yet another way this type of intuition manifests is the ability to visually perceive life forms from other dimensions. These forms might include loved ones who have passed on, spirit guides, angels, nature spirits, and others. In one Edgar Cayce reading, the recipient was told, " . . . the entity oft becomes aware of a vision within the environs or surroundings that is not of an earthly making, but is of the celestial spheres; and also of the beauty in color, and the figures that are indicated in those colors, as also music that blends with same . . . Cultivate these, for they—as the activities in the imaginative realms (should some choose to call them such)—become close akin to the real soul self . . . " (2073-2)

Psychometry is the ability to discern information

from the vibration of an object. By holding an object in one's hand, it is possible to pick up intuitive information about the object and/or the person to whom it belongs. Impressions can be received through visual images, words, thoughts, or physical sensations about the object, or through a combination of these. Insights can also come from the vibrations in a particular location or setting. Nancy shared a spontaneous experience she had with psychometry. "A week or so before Christmas, I had been meditating and praying more frequently and fervently than usual, trying to keep myself balanced so as not to succumb to the frantic commercialism of the holiday season. One day, as I took the mail from my mailbox I noticed a bright red envelope with a postmark from Australia. My friend Lucinda lived there, and I had not heard from her in two years. At the precise moment that I picked it up, I had a tremendous flash of insight and I spoke out loud the words, 'Lucinda is going to have a baby!'

"There was no reason for me to think that on a conscious level, but I hurriedly opened the envelope to see what was inside. It was a Christmas card from Lucinda and her note at the bottom was quite startling. 'By the way, we're expecting a baby in February.'"

Nancy felt that she was experiencing a heightened attunement as a result of her meditations, which allowed her to tap into the vibration of Lucinda's exciting news even before she opened the card.

Intuition Through Time
Sometimes the intuition we receive relates to a time other than the present. **Precognition** is the ability to know about something before it actually occurs. This insight into the future can happen in the conscious state as well as in the dream state, and can be experienced through any of the "clear senses" mentioned earlier. The

following example is one in which clairsentience plays a part in a precognitive experience.

Lynn shared the story of having this thought "walk" through her mind while she was driving down the street: "What would happen if a person stepped off the sidewalk into traffic?" It came out of nowhere, totally out of context of any other strains of thought, and seemed particularly odd because it was phrased in the form of a question. That was the part that caught her attention: If it hadn't been a question, she might not have even noticed it. Within two weeks, that very event occurred. While Lynn was driving down that same street, an elderly man, who was obviously disoriented, stepped out from between two cars and right into the path of her vehicle. With the recognition that "this was it," she was able to control her car and bring it quickly to a stop. In doing so, she avoided hitting the pedestrian and alerted the drivers behind her to the danger.

Retrocognition is the ability to know details about something that has taken place in the past without having been told or having read about it. As with precognition, we can experience these insights through any of the "clear senses" mentioned earlier.

Past-life memories are an example of retrocognition. The following example of past-life recall by Daniel was experienced through clairvoyance and clairsentience:

"Once while talking with several friends about the possible past-life connections among us, Ben mentioned that he felt sure that he had been a samurai warrior in Japan in a recent incarnation. To be quite honest, I had no idea what it meant to be a samurai warrior. But all of a sudden, a curtain fell in front of my eyes, showing an immense vista in front of me, like the first few seconds of a dramatic feature film. It was a lush green valley with stark mountains in the distance—a scene I have never seen before or since. I had the feeling of movement, of the wind hitting my face, and of traveling a long distance at great speed. I couldn't tell if we were on foot or horseback, but my friend Ben was definitely one of my traveling companions in what I could only assume was Japan. In that brief moment, I understood the easy camaraderie that existed between us."

Recognizing Intuitive Insights

How do we know when we are receiving intuitive information? How do we discern that particular type of information from the thousands of impulses we receive every day? As with the different types of information experienced by individuals, confirmations of intuition come to us in a variety of ways. Many people, especially those whose intuitive strength is through clairsentience, experience physical sensations that are harbingers of truth. If the impressions are of a warning nature, the physical indicators might include restlessness, physical pain, or discomfort in the stomach. Positive insights might trigger "goose bumps," a spinning sensation at the top of the head, spontaneous tears, warmth in the hands or at the base of the spine, or a sense of opening in the heart area.

Other people experience the existence of intuitive information through the emotions, such as a feeling of uneasiness, concern, or confusion. When the information is of a positive nature, joy, euphoria, or profound peace may prevail. Another indicator of intuitive information is a sense of great clarity, whether the insight comes as a thought, impression, voice, or vision.

Intuitive Development: Purpose and Intent

Hugh Lynn Cayce, eldest son of Edgar Cayce, worked a great deal with the material in the readings, particularly that which covered the inner workings of psychic abilities. After many years of interacting with Search for God study group members and experimenting with various ways of developing his own intuition, Hugh Lynn concluded that there are three valuable outcomes of developing intuitive attunement:

- *Improved communications.* When we learn to use our intuition in positive ways, a greater understanding of the motivations, thoughts, and feelings of others may result. This allows us to become more tolerant, accepting, and loving toward them.
- *Unleashed creativity.* Intuitive insights motivate us to grow closer to the creative source, thereby igniting our own creative spark and expression, which is the essence of our true self.
- *Healing of others and ourselves.* As we attune to the highest within ourselves and feel motivated to help humanity, we open ourselves to the One Force and allow its healing energy to operate through us.

Diversions on the Intuitive Path

Fear

If we all have access to intuition, information that would help us live happier, more creative, and fulfilled lives, what is it that keeps us from tuning in to, recognizing, and benefiting from it? Without a doubt, the greatest impediment to effectively working with and understanding our own intuitive strengths is *fear*. It can take many forms: fear of what others might think; fear of looking foolish; fear of making a mistake; fear of the unknown; fear of consequences; fear of losing control. The list goes on.

Fear is that element in the character and in the experience of individuals which brings about more of trouble than any other influence in the experi-

ence of an entity. For, when ye are sure of the right
path and follow it, ye do not fear. 2560-1

Our fears can lead us into a state of denial, where we
do not even recognize the promptings of our intuition
when it tries to gain our attention. When we let these
fears take hold, we are closing ourselves off from the
greatest source of insight, help, and comfort that we
have available to us.

If we let the voices of others speak louder, whether
they are our closest friends and relatives of today or the
authoritarian voices and childhood tauntings of years
past, we give them greater power than our own insights.
This Cayce reading describes what takes place when we
allow this to happen.

Here we have the experience of an entity through
the years, because of what others say, constantly
submerging that which has ever been the real interest of the entity: Intuition, things psychic, myster-
ies and such activities. Had the body, through these
years not allowed what others said to influence the
body to keep this intuition out of the life, much
greater would have been the development of the
body. 5124-1

Janice shared an experience in which her fears nearly
overrode her intuition regarding the purchase of a used
car. Because she was aware that she was letting fear take
precedence, she found a way to work through it and take
action instead of remaining immobilized:

"I needed to replace my ten-year-old, unreliable car. I
searched the local dealerships and newspapers while
researching information on the makes and models of the
vehicles I was seeing.

"One evening, I test-drove a compact sedan, and as I

tooled around the neighborhood, I felt an opening in my heart. I was really excited about the car, as it seemed a good fit. I had it assessed by my mechanic, then contacted the bank about a loan. Every time I thought about the car and the people I was buying it from, it felt right. Then fears crept in, and I became obsessed with 'what ifs': What if my intuition is wrong, and there's something better out there for me? What if I get this car now, and then find what I *really* wanted at an unbelievable price? What if I don't get this car, and my old one completely falls apart? What if I'm not able to sell my old car? What if my friends don't like it? I was driving myself crazy.

"Finally, I asked in prayer what I should do, as I was finding it difficult to remember my positive intuitive response while all these fears were holding court. The thought came to mind to work with an exercise I had learned many years before in Lucia Capacchione's book, *The Power of Your Other Hand.* This exercise is intended to help give voice to the unexpressed emotions and impressions that influence our self-image, self-esteem, and behavior. I began by writing, with my dominant hand, questions regarding how I felt about the car and the situation in general. With my nondominant hand, I wrote the responses, a process that helps to disengage normal rational thought and allows suppressed or forgotten thoughts and emotions to come to the surface.

"After a few questions, the voice that came through in my writing was that of my inner child, to whom I had paid little attention over the years. What I learned was that she was afraid that if I purchased this car, I would pay even less attention to her need for expression, that is, *my* need to play, be lighthearted, and to laugh. The car that I was considering was very different from the sport utility vehicle that *she* wanted but I couldn't afford. So, my inner child felt ignored and fought back by creating confusion.

"Because of the writing exercise, I was able to mentally tune in to my inner child and made a commitment to take care of my need for excitement and play. Then I went out and purchased the car, which has served me very well."

Low Self-Esteem

If allowing fears to take hold can be so detrimental to our development, why do we let it happen? Why do fears take precedence over our inner knowledge? One reason is low self-esteem. We forget that we are children of God, divine beings with a divine inheritance who have direct access to all the help and guidance we need. We doubt our own ability to be in touch with our higher self, or that it even exists. We enfold ourselves in thoughts and feelings that disguise our true nature. The litany of self-effacement sounds something like, "I'm not good enough," "I'm not worthy," "I don't know how," "I can't . . . " When we lend energy to such thoughts, we feed our fears rather than the divine spark within and thus dull our senses to the messages we might otherwise receive.

Perhaps our Western culture's emphasis on acquired knowledge is partly to blame. Most of us spend many years in school. In traditional institutions, we collect information in a linear, rational way, often denying our own innate knowledge. Nonlinear thinking is generally not appreciated, at best, and is frequently discouraged, either through blatant criticism or dismissive attitudes of its validity. After years of this nonsupportive response, most sensitive people learn to squelch the expression of their true feelings. Perhaps the key to integrating the inner voice with acquired knowledge is in finding ways to couch intuitive insights in more conventionally acceptable terms, allowing for an appropriate expression in any given circumstance.

Loss of Attunement or Unclear Intent

The Cayce readings are very clear that in order to tune in to our higher selves through our intuitive capabilities, we must keep spiritual growth as our primary focal point. Maintaining regular spiritual practices is absolutely essential to establishing and nourishing that attunement.

In addition to focused spiritual attunement, we need to be clear about our intent and clarifying our ideals. If we allow self-glorification, control over others, or a desire to simply make life easier to become our guiding motivation, we lose our connection to our true ideal. Most often, this creates a muddying effect on our intuitive senses, causing insights to become inaccurate or unreliable. To remain true to our higher selves, the readings suggest that unconditional love and service to others should be our guiding lights.

Pitfalls on the Intuitive Path

Judging Others

In the process of recognizing and developing our intuitive gifts, we will most likely begin to pick up information about those around us, our family, friends, co-workers, or even someone we pass on the street. It can be a great temptation to judge their thoughts, emotions, or actions, based on our insights. It is vital to seek ways that we can be of service rather than compounding another's burden through judgmentalism, reminding ourselves that there is always more to a story than we might realize.

Misinterpreting Signals

As we begin to put our intuitive insights into practice, it is likely that we will experience times when we just don't get it right. The following example, shared by Ria, is one in which the misinterpretation of an intuitive insight, compounded by judgment of another person, created a very uncomfortable and difficult situation:

"One evening after attending a conference, I was preparing for bed, anxious to get to sleep because I needed to get up early. As I was drifting off to sleep, I got the impression that I should not leave my small pack, which contained my wallet, near the bed. The feeling was very strong, but I was exhausted, and, after a moment of wondering what else to do with it, I left it where I had originally intended and just decided not to leave it unattended. I was rooming with someone I did not know well, and, although I felt a little uncomfortable with her, I decided that I was just being oversensitive and suspicious.

"The next morning, I pulled my hairbrush out of the pack and went into the bathroom, completely forgetting my resolution not to leave my belongings unattended. Then I remembered that the pack was now open on the bed in full view of my roommate, who was also getting ready. I panicked, raced back to the room, and scooped up everything that had fallen out, but could not locate the wallet. I looked *everywhere*.

"Certain that my 'intuition' had been trying to warn me about this person, I asked her if she knew the whereabouts of my wallet. When she said, 'No,' I insisted that she open her suitcase for me. I then went through her belongings. Although this response was not my normal mode of dealing with a crisis, I was filled with conviction, certain that I knew what was going on, and standing up for myself.

"My roommate was understandably confused and appalled by my actions; however, she tried valiantly to not take my behavior personally. After we both searched through each others' suitcases and other belongings, I finally found my wallet trapped in a fold of the blanket on my bed. I felt absolutely awful and incredibly ashamed.

"My first mistake had been in ignoring my intuition in the first place. If I had gone ahead and put my wallet in a more secure location, it would not have fallen out of my pack, and I would not have had to worry about it. My second mistake was that I assumed the information I was getting was about the potential behavior of my roommate, not about a situation I might create because of my suspicions. If I had taken the time to pray, to tune in a little more closely and ask for clarification, I believe I would have received the information I needed at the time. The entire episode would have been avoided."

When we allow ourselves to learn from our intuition, to move with it, and to grow with it, we truly progress—even, or perhaps especially, when we stumble and make mistakes. One person asked Cayce in a reading, "How can I avoid getting incorrect answers?" His response reflects the great compassion of the Universal Forces:

> No one way while remaining in the flesh! For, there is ever the trial, the test, the gradual growth. And there are faults, but use those faults as stepping-stones—and be guided by the greater influence that is thy ideal. 317-7

More than a simple "try, try again" approach, this answer reflects a compassionate understanding of the complexities of life on earth, and of the struggle through which *every* soul must find its way. It is almost as if the Universe is saying to us, "Okay, here you are. What have you learned? What did you miss? How might you act or respond differently the next time you are faced with a similar situation?"

Steps to Intuitive Development

Rather than a list of techniques, the following steps

come from the Cayce readings' approach, which emphasizes practices that will strengthen our connection with the Divine within and help us to better discern the information we receive:

- *Spiritual practices.* Intuition develops naturally as a result of our spiritual development. Meditating, praying, setting ideals, and working with others on a spiritual path are all important tools for spiritual growth.
- *Ask questions during meditation and listen for the answers.* If an answer isn't forthcoming, consider that there may be other underlying questions that need to be answered first.
- *Pay attention to the impressions you receive as you fall asleep or first awaken.* Insights will come as a result of asking questions during meditation, through inner reflection, or as you are falling asleep. Write these down, and find a positive way to act on them.
- *Trust your inner self as much as your analytical self.* This can take practice, as it is easy to brush aside our intuitive promptings. Give yourself permission to give voice to the intuitive.
- *Have an insatiable curiosity.* Discover those things you are drawn to and follow them.
- *Inspirational writing after a period of meditation or attunement.* While in the meditative state, write down your thoughts, feelings, and impressions.
- *Spend time in nature.* We can learn about our own natural balance and harmony by attuning to those primordial aspects of God's creation.
- *Exercise regularly and maintain a healthy diet.* If the physical body is not in equilibrium, our intuitive development is inhibited.
- *Listen to uplifting music and read inspiring literature.* This positive engagement of our mental and emotional selves nourishes us spiritually.
- *Develop your creative imagination.* Spend time

expressing talents and activities for which you have a passion.

Conclusion

Intuitive awareness is more than just an indicator of how adept we are at accessing psychic perceptions. It is an indication of how attuned we are to our spiritual side. When we develop and rely on our abilities, discern inner truths, and apply that awareness on the physical level, we open the doorway to manifesting our true highest selves.

Trust more and more in the intuitive forces, that will be the directing power through that received in the meditation with thy Maker. 257-92

3

APPLYING DREAM GUIDANCE

Whether the body desires or not, in sleep the consciousness physically is laid aside. As to what will be that it will seek, depends upon what has been builded as that it would associate itself with, physically, mentally, spiritually . . . 5754-3

THROUGHOUT THE CAYCE READINGS, emphasis is placed on the vital connection between the dreamer and the dream. What we think, feel, and do in our daily lives is reflected in our dreams and is part of the interpretation process. Dreams are conduits of information that arise simultaneously from different levels of our awareness. On one level they can be a reiteration of activities experienced during the day; while at another, deeper level, dreams frequently highlight the internal processes, emotions, or attitudes of which we might not be consciously aware. Dreams can also show us what we aren't expressing or need to express in a given situation. Simone shared a dream that clearly illustrates this point. Her dream involved a co-worker, Michael, with whom she was having difficulty. They were members of their company's software development team, in which openness and mutual support helped to spark and nurture the creative process. Michael's manner was often cold and distant, leading Simone to feel that he disliked her. It was an uncomfortable feeling that eventually inhibited the creative process so much it nearly broke down the team's progress entirely.

In the dream, Simone saw herself entering a meeting room where Michael sat alone. He appeared to be very troubled, and Simone felt a strong urge to put her arm around him and give him words of encouragement. As she did so, his face seemed to soften, and she felt an enormous sense of gratitude emanating from him. He smiled and thanked her for helping him.

When she saw Michael the following day, Simone decided to follow through with the impulse evoked by the dream. She gently asked if things were going all right for him and was surprised when he responded openly, disclosing serious family issues that had been weighing on his mind. She recognized that she had misconstrued his preoccupation with family concerns as dislike for her. After that brief interaction, they established a positive, supportive work relationship and friendship. By acting on the message of her dream, they were both helped tremendously.

Simone's willingness to follow through illustrates the positive impact of applying dream guidance in our daily lives. The Cayce readings admonish us repeatedly that "knowledge not used is sin." In a very real sense, by not following the insights we are given, whether they come through dreams or other avenues, we are limiting our potential for soul growth. This prevents our being channels of blessings to others. On the contrary, by establishing a pattern of positive action as a response to intuitive promptings, we create the potential for growth in our own lives as well as in our relationships with others.

Dreams and Ideals

. . . this ability of sleep and sense, or a sixth sense, just what, how, may this knowledge be used to advantage for an individual's development towards that it would attain?

As to how it may be used, then, depends upon what is the ideal of that individual; for . . . if the ideal of the individual is lost, then the abilities for that faculty or . . . sense of an individual to contact the spiritual forces are gradually lost, or barriers are builded that prevent . . . a sensing of the nearness of an individual to a spiritual development. 5754-3

When circumstances in our lives become complicated, our decision-making processes can seem unreliable at best. At such times, we need to focus and redirect our energy into a specific and positive ideal. As the excerpt from the reading above states so clearly, "if the ideal of the individual is lost, then the abilities . . . to contact the spiritual forces are gradually lost . . . "

Daniel had been questioning his relationship with Anna, who was recently divorced from her husband. He prayed and meditated daily, asking for guidance. Although Daniel felt very close to Anna on a spiritual level, he sought to understand the deeper purpose of their bond and to cope with the difficult elements of the relationship, which included geographical distance and a rather negative response from Anna's children. These complexities caused him to wonder if he should continue to pursue this potentially meaningful relationship.

In a dream, Daniel saw himself getting on a bus with Anna. As they moved to the back seat, they became lovingly entwined, almost as if they were one person. As the dream continued, her son approached them, saying, "You can't replace my father." Daniel responded, "Wherever there is love, it's good, and there is something positive and encouraging to be learned." He acknowledged the love between the boy and his father and the value of love in that relationship. At the same time, he felt encouraged to pursue his connection with Anna, since the dream seemed to come in response to his prayers for guidance. It also reflected his highest ideal of being of service in a spirit of oneness and unconditional love.

Another dreamer found his ideal was confirmed in a dream during a time when he was struggling with strong sexual energy after a long separation from his girlfriend. Ray shared the following:

"My brother Jerry and I entered a restaurant. A co-worker came up from the basement. I told him that we stopped in to meditate but I couldn't get my brother interested in trying it. Jerry ordered a wild wolf dinner. I ordered the goose dinner."

In this dream, Jerry represented the physical side of Ray. The wolf entree and disinterest in meditation indicated giving in to his sexual urges. The symbology of the goose dinner which Ray chose represented oneness and fidelity, based partially on the following readings' quote:

Once united . . . relationships are to be as one . . . Man may learn a great deal from a study of the goose . . . Once it has mated, never is there a mating with any other—either the male or female, no matter how soon the destruction of the mate may occur . . . 826-6

This dream symbol reassured Ray that he was in attunement with his ideal.

It is amazing how much information we can discern by maintaining a constant attunement with the highest part of ourselves. This is noted in the following question asked of Edgar Cayce and his response:

> (Q) Please advise the body as to how he may best gain control of himself and utilize his abilities to best advantage.
>
> (A) Depend more upon the intuitive forces from within and not harken so much to that of outside influences—but learn to listen to that still small voice from within, remembering . . . not in the storm, the lightning, nor in any of the loud noises . . . made to attract man, but rather in the still small voice . . . does the impelling influence come to life in an individual . . . which must be the basis of human endeavor; for without the ability to constantly hold before self the ideal . . . man becomes as one adrift, pulled hither and yon by the various calls . . . of those who would give of this world's pleasure in fame, fortune, or what not. 239-1

Cosmic Pats on the Back

Some dreams serve as a confirmation that our daily actions are in keeping with God's will, even when we may be burdened by doubts. Kathy shared how self-doubts about her abilities as a single mother were beginning to take their toll. She had started to think that her four teenagers had no direction in life and that, worse, they didn't love one another. This perception was particularly painful for her, since she had tried very hard over the years to instill a sense of appreciation and love in her children, especially toward each other.

Kathy prayed and meditated often during this stressful time and received encouragement in the form of a dream. In it, she saw her four children riding together in a car which was surrounded by a beautiful golden light. They were singing and laughing together, obviously enjoying each others' company. Oddly enough, each child had his or her own steering wheel even though they all were riding in the same vehicle and headed down the same road. The love they felt for one another was apparent, and the whole dream conveyed a sense of joy and oneness.

The message of the dream was clear. Although it was not always apparent in their day-to-day lives, the dream showed clearly that Kathy's children cared deeply for one another. She felt that the light around the car signified God's protection, renewing her confidence that they were all right. That each child had a separate steering wheel symbolized their individuality. Each was finding and following a personal path, while ultimately all were headed in the same direction. This was very reassuring to Kathy, as she felt it to be a true portrayal and realized that her fears, while understandable, had been unfounded.

Keep in mind that just because a dream deals with one's daily routine and doesn't seem particularly glamorous or intriguing, it still can be quite valuable in bringing us closer to fulfilling our purpose in life. As the following quote points out, it is essential that we value what may appear as insignificant occurrences and the supposedly "unimportant" choices we make:

> For, it is the one who is not too severe in *any* manner that achieves the most—rather in God's way; little by little, here a little, there a little, line upon line, precept upon precept, rather than hoping for some great deed that may be accomplished in a

moment . . . *live* the life! *Be* what you are . . . 3084-1

Sometimes our dreams simply confirm the path we've chosen to follow, like a cosmic pat on the back for a choice well made. This brings to mind the dream Sherry had when she decided to end a long-standing but stagnant romantic relationship. Their paths of growth had diverged years before, yet they were still together out of habit. After much agonizing over the consequences of breaking up, Sherry finally found the courage to say goodbye. The night after making her decision, she had a short, poignant dream in which she saw herself working diligently in an overgrown garden, pulling up an abundance of weeds by the roots. Although it was hard work, Sherry felt an enormous sense of satisfaction with each weed pulled. The most telling part of the dream was the huge smile that was on her face all the while. What a sense of relief and reassurance she felt when she awoke! That overgrown garden clearly represented her unproductive relationship. And the liberating freedom she felt while weeding confirmed that she had made the right decision.

Dreams in Sequence

It can be extremely helpful to examine together recurring or related dreams for the insights they offer on the same question. Jocelyn was a new college graduate who was confused about which career path to follow. Although she had a B.A. in English, it was her double minor in education and journalism which seemed to be causing a pull in two different career directions. She had completed student teaching and felt confident that she could easily handle teaching the high school subject matter. She found it difficult, however, to deal with the lethargy and lack of enthusiasm many of the students showed toward learning, and she was not sure she could tolerate their indifference. Jocelyn really enjoyed writing and editing and had wondered whether a career in newswriting for television or radio might be a better choice. Two dreams she experienced within days of one another addressed her dilemma. In the first dream, Jocelyn was in a classroom with a group of fourteen year olds. She was surprised by the fact that they seemed quite cooperative and were noticeably more focused than the exasperating students she had encountered during her student teaching. Jocelyn commented to herself during this dream, "I guess I really could do this if I wanted to."

Two days later, she dreamed she was standing on a beach when newsman Dan Rather walked up to her. They began to kiss; and, although it was a pleasant encounter, she realized that she cared for her boyfriend more and really wanted to be with him. Dan Rather asked her what she planned to do with her future. She replied, "I'm not quite sure," to which he responded, "Well, just remember, Jocelyn, you're a very talented and gifted person, and there's a lot that you can do with your life."

She felt encouraged by the praise she had received from such an accomplished television anchorperson and more clear about her commitment to her boyfriend. Combined, these dreams gave Jocelyn some clear guidance about her innermost feelings regarding her career. The first dream seemed to be assuring her that if she chose to follow the path of teaching, her experience would be more pleasant than anticipated. It also reaffirmed her ability to convey the material effectively to receptive students. However, there didn't seem to be a great deal of enthusiasm on her part for this choice.

In the second dream, a more expansive environment implied wider career horizons. The glamour of meeting a well-known person (who obviously represents the world of media) created a very different feeling from the first dream. The act of kissing implied a unity with the career that Mr. Rather symbolized, suggesting that the more fulfilling career path would be found in following her heart's desire.

An added key to understanding this dream is in the play on words found in Dan Rather's name—what would she *rather* do? He asked her about her plans for the future, and Jocelyn's expression of uncertainty reflected the actual emotions she was experiencing in her conscious life. This dream also gave her needed reassurance that her abilities are considerable and her options many. It was an uplifting, inspiring ending to a dream that will help her move forward with clarity and confidence, whatever course she takes.

Dreams Relating to Health

Dreams can also serve as indicators or warnings regarding our physical health, providing general assessment as well as guidance on how to address a particular ailment. For example, a dream about gorging on desserts might suggest reevaluating current dietary trends. A car out of gas may prompt the dreamer to take some action to increase physical energy, and so on.

Kimberly shared a dream that seemed to come in response to a concern about her menstrual cycle, which had become erratic. She wondered one evening if she ought to seek medical attention. That night she had a dream in which she saw herself on her hands and knees, scrubbing the kitchen floor with a bucket and brush. She interpreted the image to mean that her body was simply "cleaning house," and that the situation would be corrected naturally, which it was.

Often parents receive this type of information for the

children in their care, as the following example illustrates:

Meredith was concerned about the fact that her eight-year-old daughter Amy was not gaining weight properly. She had taken Amy to three different doctors; all had different opinions about Amy's condition, and none was able to provide advice that was ultimately successful. Meredith was an active member of a prayer-for-healing group at the time, and she asked the group to pray for her daughter regarding this concern.

After having done what she "knew" to do, as Cayce suggests, by seeking medical advice and requesting prayer assistance, Meredith had a dream. In it, she was standing on the stairwell of A.R.E.'s headquarters building, looking out over the patio area. There was an enormous crater in the patio, lined with long, vertical pipes similar to those of a pipe organ. Members of the prayer group were inside the crater. Meredith yelled to one of the group members, "What are you doing?" His response came back, "Oh, we're polishing the pipes; it's the apple juice that tarnishes them." That was the end of the dream.

At that time, Amy was known as the "Apple Juice Kid"—she was *constantly* drinking apple juice. Meredith recognized that the members of her prayer group represented a caring and trusted symbol for healing, and she immediately restricted Amy's apple juice consumption. Within a short time, Amy started to gain weight and felt an increase in energy.

The Cayce readings state that *anything* that is helpful to the body can also be harmful when taken in excess. Meredith felt that the dream was telling her that Amy's constant apple juice intake had created an adverse reaction in her digestive system (the pipes). For both of them, it was the answer to prayer, and something, as Meredith said, "the doctors would *never* have known to suggest."

Our interrelationships with one another can also allow us to have dreams for others. Such was the case for Richard. One day his office mate Margaret described a very uncomfortable pain she was experiencing throughout her right side. Richard then recalled his previous night's dream. In it Margaret described the pain to him and told him that Japanese green tea would help ease the discomfort. She asked Richard if he had any or if he knew anyone who did. Richard did not have the tea, but he volunteered to canvass his co-workers to see if anyone else did. He found someone who had tea that was similar, but not specifically that tea. The dream ended with Margaret telling him that it had to be Japanese green tea.

Richard had lived in Japan and was familiar with the language and culture. When he remembered the dream, he phoned a Japanese friend to see if she had that tea. She did have Japanese tea, but, as foretold in the dream, it was not the traditional green variety. He continued his search until he found the correct one.

Margaret drank the tea and soon experienced a marked decrease in pain, enabling her to sleep comfortably. Later, medical tests could not diagnose the condition, but fortunately the pain eventually subsided entirely.

Communication with Loved Ones

Dreams frequently bridge the gap between the physical plane and spiritual realms, allowing us to communicate with loved ones who have passed on. These dreams bring reassurance that the soul is eternal and that our connections to one another never really die.

Denise shared this experience following her father's death.

"A few weeks after my dad died, two longtime family friends told my mother that they were sure they had seen my father. Sheila was in a grocery store when a man approached her and struck up a conversation. When she turned to speak to him, she realized that it was my father. She was so shocked that she could hardly speak and hurried out of the store. She was so upset that her husband remarked, 'Goodness, you look like you've seen a ghost!'

"The other friend was our neighbor Oscar, who drove past Mom's house early one afternoon and saw a man sitting on the porch. He was concerned about my mother's welfare and decided to investigate. As he walked across the yard, he stopped as he realized, 'My heavens, that's Tom!' Just as he formed that thought, the person on the porch dematerialized, disappearing right in front of his eyes.

"Since both my mother and I believe that my father is alive in spirit and that it may be possible to see him under the right circumstances, we began to feel a little hurt that he hadn't appeared to us. For weeks after I heard of these encounters, I studied passersby to see if I might catch a glimpse of Dad. I even asked out loud, 'Why won't you show yourself to me?'

"Then, one night I had this dream. I was at a party in a home I didn't recognize. I went into the kitchen where several people were standing around and talking. As I walked toward the refrigerator, I noticed a man sitting on a stool facing away from me. When I got within a few feet of him, he spun around and I realized it was my dad! As he looked at me, he was smiling, practically beaming, and seemed so happy. I took one look at him and fainted! At least, I think I fainted; my knees went out from under me and the room went dark. And I said to myself in the dream, 'You fainted! How could you do that? It's a dream!'

"When I woke up, I realized that I certainly wasn't ready for such an encounter, that if I came upon him by surprise in a dream and fainted, it definitely could have been devastating if I had seen him on the street somewhere. I think that's what he was trying to tell me. I was thankful for the experience, and I continue to meet my dad from time to time in the dream world."

In the following dream, Rita, whose husband had recently passed away, gained comfort and assurance that, although he was no longer with her, he was being taken care of in the spiritual realm:

"I was pushing Alfred in a wheelchair. We had to travel quite a way on a path with twists and turns. While we went along, a friend tried to move Alfred out of the chair and get into the chair himself. I finally addressed this person and said, 'This is not for you. Find your own.' Alfred and I continued on; the way became straighter. We arrived at a Union. Alfred rose out of the wheelchair and walked inside; I followed. The woman at the counter welcomed him and said, 'Oh, your position is on the next level. Just go up those stairs. Here are your keys.' Alfred looked at me and waved. The clerk then said, 'You can have a set of keys, too,' and I replied, 'No, not yet.' I walked outside into a garden. The wheelchair had disappeared. I was very peaceful and excited because the atmosphere was beautiful. The people were preparing food for lunch, and I knew that Alfred would be loved and well taken care of by everyone. I knew he would be fine, but I also knew that whenever I wanted 'my keys,' they were waiting for me."

Lucid Dreams

According to G. Scott Sparrow's book *Lucid Dreaming: Dawning of the Clear Light*, lucid dreaming simply means "the experience of becoming aware that one is dreaming while in the dream." One positive way to integrate a higher level of thinking into our daily actions is by learning to sustain the lucid state while in waking consciousness. As Cayce suggested, we can "stand aside and watch self go by," creating an objectivity that allows us to break free of self-imposed limitations. That freedom of objective choice then expands our emotional and mental awareness to a level of intuitive understanding that, in turn, releases a totally new response. That lucid response is true creativity.

Marion shared a technique she used to deal constructively with a horrifying lucid dream that recurred frequently. Marion grew up in Europe during World War II and, as a small child, had been interred in a concentration camp with her family. Although she survived the atrocities of the concentration camp, the anxiety and fear of that experience remained with her. This is her description of the dream:

"I am walking down a pathway past a building surrounded by barbed-wire fences. As I approach the building, which looks extremely similar to the concentration camp from my childhood, I begin to feel more and more fearful. I am afraid because I know they are going to take me inside there. The reason they're going to take me in is because I don't have a means of transportation. At this point, I become lucid, realizing that I'm dreaming; however, because I am still frightened by the awful scene, I wake up screaming, unable to calm down for quite some time."

Marion's husband had a very good suggestion for working with this traumatic dream. He recommended that, since she usually became lucid in the dream, she could alleviate her dilemma by "dreaming up" a means of escape. In that way, she could transform the helplessness she felt upon recognizing the inevitable, terrifying outcome of the dream.

She soon had an opportunity to take her husband's advice. As the dream unfolded once again, she became lucid as she neared the barbed-wire fence; but instead of her normal fear response, Marion recognized her ability to take a more positive course of action. She created in her dream a means of transportation which, quite appropriately, turned out to be a tricycle! She hopped on the tricycle, rode away from the oppressive scene, and never had that dream again!

The symbol of the tricycle makes perfect sense since she had been little more than a toddler when the imprisonment had occurred. What Marion did was allow herself to release her fear-based response to the dream images and instead take action that was both empowering and constructive. She woke up feeling free of the lifelong fear which had clouded so many of her thoughts and dreams.

Not all lucid dreams offer such a direct solution to a challenging situation, but it's important to remember that we can control our own attitudes and behavior to a certain degree, whether in the sleep state or in conscious life. Marion's sincere desire to transform the negative feelings of her real-life experience was crucial in enabling her to integrate the sense of peace and serenity of her waking life into the deep unconscious of her dreams. Marion had also discovered that by taking the time to pray, meditate, and work seriously to understand the patterns of her own dreams, she could take a giant leap forward on her path to wholeness and spiritual growth.

For many people, the sensation of flying triggers the realization that they are dreaming. In fact, any occurrence that is outside our normal realm of capability can serve as a precursor to lucidity.

Robert had a series of lucid dreams throughout his childhood and adolescence which mirrored his need for emotional freedom and enhanced his perception of his ordinary surroundings.

"I remember that in the dreams I would fly around our

farm, around the orchard, back by the corn patch and chicken runs. I knew I was dreaming and was very excited about the fact that I was flying. I wasn't high, just a few feet off the ground where my youngster's eye level would have been. Details that I had never seen before would pop out in the dreams, colors were brighter, and everything seemed intensified. I would look at this side of the tree and see the sap formation or would notice the light refracting off the fence in a certain way. Later, when awake, I would go out and actually find these different things that I had dreamed about . . . What I thought about in these dreams was that while I was flying, I was in a space where I wanted to be—just free to be myself, which was very rare on our farm. Wandering aimlessly was not thought of highly, as there were always chores to do."

This dream illustrates some common elements of lucid dreams. It enhanced Robert's perception of everyday reality and evoked a state of mindfulness, taking him a step further in recognizing and appreciating the beauty all around him.

During the 1970s, Scott Sparrow and Mark Thurston, author and psychologist, formulated a lucid dream induction strategy. They believed that an ideal way to prompt lucidity was to have individuals relive a previous dream "with full awareness that the experience is only a fantasy." Dr. Sparrow's article, "How to Induce Lucid Dreams" (July/August 1986, *Venture Inward* magazine) explains how this process gave participants the opportunity to respond to the initial dream in a more creative way. " . . . reliving the dream in a 'lucid' frame of mind would:

- "Help the [dreamer] work through 'unfinished business' from the first dream.
- "Instill the idea that one always has the capacity to respond to dream encounters in a variety of ways.

- "Serve as a rehearsal for becoming more aware—even lucid—in subsequent dreams."

Carlos Castaneda recommended giving yourself the presleep suggestion to look at your hands in your dream. When you see them, the awareness that you are dreaming is triggered. Sustaining that perception of your hands may also prolong the lucid state.

In the same vein, Sparrow suggests formulating a meaningful affirmation or phrase to repeat at the moment of becoming lucid. The dreamer can go a step further by asking to be guided wherever she/he can be of the greatest service at that moment.

Past-Life Dreams

Past-life dreams can have a tremendous impact on our understanding of current circumstances and relationships in our lives. If it's true that we bring with us past talents, inclinations, and life lessons, then it's logical that those influences would present themselves in the dream state. More attention is given in a later chapter to the ways that we can apply insights gained from memories of other lifetimes, but here are some guideposts for recognizing reincarnation dreams:

- Settings or dress from other time periods, e.g., armor signifying a medieval incarnation or a toga representing a Roman one
- Speaking or hearing others speak in a foreign language
- Exceptional vividness (feeling, color, clarity)
- Sense of being immersed in a different culture
- Seeing or knowing dates in the past
- Sense of looking back in time, perhaps to another era
- Floating sensation; being suspended over the scene and observing

- Feeling oneself to be in a different body
- Recognizing current friends and family as distinct characters in past-life circumstances

Here's an example of a past-life dream that was eventually verified for Nancy, giving her helpful insight into her career path and several current relationships:

"In this dream, I had the sensation of floating above the scene, suspended about six feet in the air, looking down at the huge wooden door of a beautiful cathedral. In front of the door was a tour group in modern-day clothes. I knew that the location was England. As the dream progressed, I became a part of the scene, walked through the door, and found myself in another time period, perhaps the sixteenth or seventeenth century. Immediately, I recognized my sister from my present life. She appeared as a young man dressed in a cleric's garb. I knew that I was part of life at the cathedral and that she and I were close friends. I watched as offerings were made at a beautiful altar, with sunlight streaming through the stained-glass windows.

"In the next scene, I was in what seemed to be a rectory or office. I sat at a desk that I knew was mine and looked up to see two co-workers from my waking life dressed as deacons of the church. One of them proceeded to ask me questions and to write my answers on a blackboard. He asked, 'In which countries did you have past-life experiences that are now impacting this lifetime?' I answered, '... England, obviously, Japan, Greece, France, and China.' He then said, 'Ah, China, now there's a lifetime I'd like you to express more of!'

"I felt as I awoke that it had been a very positive and fulfilling period for me."

This dream inspired Nancy to continue on a spiritual path for the sake of her soul development as well as her life's work. She was quite awestruck when, three months later, she literally found herself in England, in front of

Salisbury Cathedral looking at that same tour group and wooden door she had viewed in her dream. She had an overwhelming sensation of having been there before and became extremely emotional when she saw the church entrance. It was almost as if she had come home from a long journey. She realized not only the accuracy of her precognitive dream, but also how it appeared to confirm a past-life experience there.

Nancy's visit to England evoked a clearer understanding of her connection to the various characters in the dream as well as of her innate attraction to the cultures mentioned. She was particularly fascinated with the mention of China, since she has always had a strong desire to visit there one day.

Precognitive Dreams

Perhaps the most frequently asked question regarding dreams is, "How do I really know whether or not my dreams are predictive?"

The simple answer is, "You never truly know for sure." But that doesn't mean you can't take all the measures possible to alleviate the impact of the dream's outcome (if it's negative) by applying some of the dream's suggestions in your waking state. It's also good to keep in mind the Cayce readings' suggestion that dreams that recur more than three times indicate a strong likelihood that it is predictive.

Barbara told of a dream she had one December night, in which she and her husband were conversing while standing in the house they were in the process of buying. Upon awakening, Barbara had in her mind the date February 2. She didn't know what that might relate to, because their closing date was set for mid-January; but she marked her calendar so that she would pay attention when that day arrived. Two weeks later, she received a call from her Realtor, who apologized and said that the house would not be available until February 2. Barbara soon realized, "Oh my gosh, that was the date in my dream!"

We can see that such confirmations give credence to the path we've chosen to take. In Barbara's case, this incident allowed her to feel that the delay was all right and that she had chosen the right house. She and her husband ended up buying the "dream" house.

A dream that Beth had emphasizes our interconnectedness with one another, not only with family members, but in the workplace as well.

"I was traveling out of town on a business trip. A colleague was scheduled to present technical data during a seminar in the home-office city. The night before the actual presentation was to occur, I had the following dream:

"I dreamed that I was accompanying one of my co-workers, Adam, as he was preparing to make a presentation to a large audience. We were seated side-by-side in the auditorium as people began to come into the room. I began to sense a bit of nervousness from Adam as he composed himself and his material. He was ordinarily comfortable speaking to crowds since he held impeccable qualifications in his profession. In the dream scene . . . we sat together for a few moments. Then it was his time to get up and go to the podium. He walked forward and just as he was about to reach the podium area, he collapsed. This caused a commotion in the room, and I moved forward to check if Adam was okay. I noticed that certain people were snickering over what had happened, intimating that he had been carelessly drinking or something . . . to cause the fall. I was angry with their misinterpretation, and I told them not to snicker but rather to focus their thoughts on what they had come for: information. I then noticed another co-worker, Joe, take

Adam's place at the podium with the presentation material.

"Upon awakening . . . I experienced a chilling sensation that seemed to snap me into alertness. For me, that's a signal that the message is precognitive. It's a very distinct coldness that moves through me, removing distraction, bringing extreme focus.

"When I called the office the following afternoon, they told me that Adam had had a seizure and was unable to make the presentation. Joe had taken his place. As the dream had indicated, a few co-workers inaccurately suspected that he was suffering from too much partying. As it turned out, a tumor had caused the seizure. The dream served as a reminder to maintain a clear focus on my purpose and to avoid petty distraction."

The next dream touches upon a variety of elements that can be present in psychic dreams. Lawrence's recurring childhood dreams were a good indication that his dream information was of great importance. The strong emotional impact that he had when he awoke from such dreams implied that Lawrence was receiving warnings. In retrospect, it's easy to recognize the preparation these repetitive images afforded him for later life-threatening circumstances.

"At age six, I awoke in the middle of the night, too terrified to scream. I was covered in nervous sweat and had a horrible taste in my mouth. It was the first nightmare I ever had, and it reoccurred three or four times a year at first, but gradually dwindled to once every eighteen months or so as I reached puberty.

"In the dream, I was laid out naked on a cold table, shivering and embarrassed. There was a bright light above me and, although I could see no wires, I felt that I was attached to one on the inside of my body. Someone was tugging at it as if I were a puppet with internal strings. I could sense a drip, drip, drip coming from the lights, but there was no sound. The room was slowly rotating, as if on a turntable. I heard muffled sounds as if someone were talking under water. At first it was all very slow and rhythmical.

"Although I was freezing on the outside and wanted a blanket, I was getting hotter and hotter on the inside. There was a rusty taste in my mouth, and I wanted to spit but could not. My heart beat faster and faster, until I thought it would burst out of my skin. As the dream progressed, all these music-videolike images would speed up faster and faster, and I would wake up.

"At first the dream came frequently, and it made such a terrifying impression on me that I would wake up as soon as it began again. Months could have gone by, but like a familiar tune, I knew immediately at the first visual note that it was about to recur. One of my biggest memories of puberty was the fact that the dream *stopped;* from the ages of fourteen to twenty-two, the dream completely subsided. By age twenty-three, I had totally put it out of my head.

"Then, the day before I was to run my first marathon, as I stepped out of a taxi, my legs gave way, and I fell into the street. My whole left side was semiparalyzed. Feeling very disoriented, I went to my apartment to lie down and lost consciousness, slipping into a semicoma that lasted for seven days.

"I was eventually found by worried friends and family members, who took me to the hospital where my health continued to deteriorate. After two spinal taps, I was diagnosed with spinal meningitis *and* hepatitis. My body was shutting down rapidly. A priest came to administer the last rites before my final diagnostic test, an angiogram. Hope for my survival was pretty slim, because the meningitis had settled into the lining between my brain and skull. I was conscious enough to wonder what I had done to anger God enough to take me so young.

"I prayed as I was being wheeled down the hall for the angiogram and lost consciousness seconds later.

"Sometime in the next few minutes, it was as if my old familiar dream began once again. I recognized it right away. I was naked on a cold table, shivering and embarrassed. There was a bright light above me. I realized I was literally *living* the dream as the doctor explained to me that they were going to shoot a rusty-tasting dye into my heart, which would make me very warm. A wire would be threaded through my body and into my heart. The doctor said I might feel a tugging, like a puppet string or fishing line, inside my body, but I was not to worry. The dizziness I would feel might make the room appear to be turning, but it wouldn't be. As the drip-drip-drip of the dye went into my tubing, I became semiconscious. I already knew everything that was about to happen to me because I had dreamed it so many times! I relaxed and let the dream play out.

"When it was over, the doctors asked if I had ever had an angiogram before; they couldn't believe I went through the whole procedure with a big smile on my face. I learned later that many people have cardiac arrest during angiograms. The process involves pumping dye into the heart, which ejects it, forcing the dye out into the blood vessels. Photos are then taken to see if there are any blockages.

"I eventually made a full recovery; the doctors were amazed that there were no signs of mental or physical trauma."

Because he had previously encountered the procedure in numerous dreams, Lawrence was able to transcend the psychological and emotional shock of that extremely stressful situation.

Another very specific warning came to Lisa in a dream in which she saw herself driving on a familiar highway near her home. As she got on the exit ramp, she pulled up behind an open-bed truck that had a refrigerator on the back of it. The truck driver pulled abruptly away from the stop sign, which jerked the refrigerator, causing it to topple off the truck onto Lisa's windshield. She felt herself being crushed by the weight of the refrigerator and felt as if she were dying. She woke up screaming, and it took her several hours to recover from the emotional strain it caused.

When she recovered from her terror, Lisa wrote down the dream in detail, feeling that it conveyed an important message. Several months later, she was driving on the same familiar highway and got onto the same exit ramp, triggering her memory of the dream. There, in front of her, were the exact open-bed truck and refrigerator she had seen in her nightmare. Lisa's immediate reaction was to stop her car well behind the truck. As the truck moved away from the intersection, the refrigerator teetered and then fell off the back. Lisa would have been in the very place where the refrigerator fell if she hadn't chosen to maintain her distance. By being aware and receptive to the dream warning, she undoubtedly saved herself, if not from death, from a very serious accident.

Not all predictive dreams are this dramatic. They can, however, be extremely helpful in providing meaningful insights into daily circumstances.

The Cayce readings refer to precognitive dreams as "foreshadowing" the possible outcome of trends that we are building in our lives. What we experience in the material dimension is merely a reflection of what is being formed at a higher level. So, when we are attuned to these higher levels of consciousness, we are actually becoming aware of events that might occur in the physical future.

When Edgar Cayce was asked about the meaning of a dream in which a young woman got into a terrible argument with her new mother-in-law, he suggested that it

could certainly be predictive—if the two of them continued to hold the same attitudes about one another. In
other words, if they kept relating to one another in their
current manner, they would inevitably end up in a major argument. A helpful aspect of this reading emphasized that the daughter-in-law had the ability to alter the
outcome of the dream by changing her behavior in a
positive way. Once again, we are reminded that the future is not set in stone. By taking constructive action, we
can create different outcomes from those forewarned in
dreams.

This is illustrated profoundly in the dream experience
shared by Ellen.

"In the dream, my aunt called to say that there had
been an accident. My parents, who were on a road trip
across country, had died in the Cascade Mountains
when their car went over a cliff. My uncle was already on
his way out there from New Jersey to identify the bodies
and bring them back home. 'I love you,' my aunt said, as
she hung up the phone.

"The dream was so real, I jumped out of bed and
rushed into the dark living room, trying to get my bearings. Somehow I knew that it was Tuesday in the dream
and, as I came fully awake, I realized that today was actually Thursday.

"My parents were on a three-month journey around
the country at the time. I was house-sitting at their
home, and we had agreed that they would call every Sunday night at seven o'clock to touch base.

"I realized that this could actually be a precognitive
dream. After much thought and prayer, I decided not to
voice my concern on the phone when my parents called,
until I had a sense of where they were and what their
plans were going to be for the next few days.

"When the call came on Sunday night, they were in
Washington state. The plan was to do a little sightseeing

the next day, then to start heading for home through the Cascade Mountains. That was to be on Tuesday.

"I was frightened. Barely able to get out the words, I asked my mother if it was possible to change their route—if there was another way to get where they were headed. Mom responded, 'Yes, I think so. I'll ask your father. What's wrong?' I decided to tell her about the dream, to give them an opportunity to pray about it and make their own decision. I tried not to alarm her too much, while at the same time trying to get across the impact that the dream had on me. She promptly put my father on the phone.

"After retelling the dream to my dad, I asked him if it were possible to avoid those mountains. He said that they had actually been trying to decide between the mountain route and one that would take them through the low country, and had only decided that day to take the high road. He said that they would talk about it, but he didn't see why they couldn't change plans just to be on the safe side.

"My parents did decide to take the alternate route and eventually returned safely home."

It is impossible to say if Ellen's dream was truly predictive of a catastrophe; but one thing is certain: If she had chosen not to tell her parents about the dream and something drastic had taken place, she would have regretted her silence for many years to come.

That's not to say that every frightening dream we ever experience is warning us about a future event. What it does mean, however, is that Cayce's concept of "foreshadowing" in dreams is worthy of examination. His readings suggest that anything of real importance which happens in our lives has already been dreamed and that we are shown this information for a reason. Because we each possess free will, we have the power to redirect the trends that develop in our lives. What Ellen was shown in her dream could be viewed as a likely outcome if her parents had continued in the direction they were headed. But because Ellen recognized the devastating impact such a "trend" could have upon her parents and family, she was able to interject another alternative to that trend. Her suggestion of taking a different route was a positive way to redirect the situation. Ellen's parents evaluated her dream and their circumstances while keeping their daughter's loving input in mind. Their choice to change their plans was one that made Ellen very happy.

But how do we know if a dream is truly predictive, and does it lose importance if it's not precognitive in the traditional physical sense? We probably cannot ever be one hundred percent sure whether a dream is precognitive, but there are certain guidelines we can follow which give us a framework for understanding our personal symbols and dream images.

Repetitive dreams can signal the prediction of an event, such as in Lawrence's dramatic hospital example. One overriding occurrence that should be an attention-getter is the emotional impact that a dream has. How deep a sense of urgency or import do we feel upon awakening from a given dream? Are we rather neutral, or do we feel perplexed, concerned, or frightened, as did Lisa in her dream with the truck? To put it simply, feelings are crucial to pinpointing significant dreams.

As you become accustomed to working with dreams, you will learn to recognize the ways in which dreams clue you in to a message that is precognitive or psychic in nature. There are also universal symbols which for most people indicate a future event:

- Anything that has to do with time. A clock, calendar, or timepiece; or hearing dates or times in the dream may be significant.
- Physical proximity to an object may represent a

specific time span; for example, if an image is ten yards away, it may indicate an event perhaps ten days or ten weeks away.

- If you find yourself floating above a scene or seeing an unfamiliar place from afar, this may indicate the site of a future visit.
- A crystal ball, crystals, or other divining tools are typical predictive symbols.
- Receiving a phone call in a dream may indicate a psychic message.
- Dreams of holy places like temples, churches, or synagogues may indicate intuitive or spiritual insights.
- A guide or holy person might appear to impart wisdom, intuitive guidance, or simply lend support.
- Airplanes or airports may represent different *planes* or levels of consciousness.
- Predictive dreams are often more vivid in color or clarity than ordinary dreams, especially if you usually dream in black and white.
- Predictive dreams often have a TV screen or movie quality.

Dream Recall and Interpretation

One must be unflinchingly honest in order to interpret dreams accurately and benefit from the process. Here is a list of easily applied ways to recall dreams and to approach dream interpretation from an intuitive, right-brained perspective:

1. Keep a notepad, pen, and flashlight near the bed. Drink several glasses of water prior to bedtime.

2. Upon waking, remain still to let the dream solidify. To aid recall, move into or retain the position you were in when the dream occurred.

3. Take note of your emotional state upon waking.

4. Write down a few words about the dream's action,

symbols, or the feelings it evoked, and give it a title to help establish recall.

5. Think about the dream and reenact it during your morning routine, so that it becomes ingrained in your memory.

6. Say some of the words aloud to trigger recall or give new insight into the images, plays on words, etc.

7. Sometime later in the day, revisit the dream. Allow it to be in your consciousness.

8. Discuss your dreams with interested friends or family. Their insights can lend an objective perspective to your understanding.

9. Be aware of synchronistic events that occur related to the dream, noticing who or what triggers those events.

10. Ask specifically for clarity about the dream, and review it mentally just before sleep.

A Five-Step Approach to Integrating Dream Insights into Daily Activities

If you prefer a more structured approach to understanding your dreams, try the following steps:

• *Identify feelings.* What was the general tone of the dream? How did you feel when you woke up? What emotions did you and the characters express in the dream? Try to sense the overall nature of the dream before delving into details. (It is always good to evaluate your feelings upon awakening whether you remember the dream or not.)

• *Specify a theme.* What was the essential plot of the dream? Record a brief statement, if possible, focusing on the *activity* in the dream. What happened? Don't be concerned so much with when it happened, but identify the action itself. What is the dream's essence?

A theme is similar to a story outline. A single dream

might have several themes, especially if it is long or includes a number of scenes. Refrain from attempting an interpretation just yet. Instead of referring to specific people or objects in the dream, use "someone" or "something," e.g., "Something is preventing someone from getting somewhere."

- *Compile a list of symbols.* Try to look at the dream symbols from a broad, open-minded perspective, eliminating preconceptions about objects or people. Answer some basic questions about what the symbols mean to you. Perhaps create your own dream dictionary, considering these questions: (1) What is it? (2) What does it do/ look like? (3) If a person, since people often represent aspects of yourself, (a) What is this person's occupation? (b) What does she/he represent to me? (c) What is the first thing that comes to mind when I think of this person? (4) What do you like/dislike about the object or person? (5) Are there plays on words or names? For example, Jane Fonda could mean "fond" of someone.

- *Correlate the insights with personal reality.* See how this dream relates to something that's occurring in your conscious life right now. After following the previous steps, what is your basic understanding of the insights you've gathered so far? Settle on at least one level of understanding, knowing that more clarification may come later. Be patient.

- *Apply what you've learned.* Look for any ways, no matter how simple, that you can *use* the insights gained from the dream. Compose a realistic, practical statement describing what you believe the dream is saying and how you can deal with the issue in your daily life; e.g., "My dream tells me I get too easily angered by my children. I will make a conscious effort to be more patient, perhaps by counting to ten before reacting to my children's actions or modifying my attitude toward them in some positive way." Once you have chosen a course of action, and this final step has been put into practice, you will either receive further guidance and maybe a clarifying dream or the situation/issue presented will begin to change and resolve itself through the action taken.*

Conclusion

Dreams speak to us in an endless variety of ways: foretelling of potential occurrences, offering health insights, illuminating past-life relationships, providing needed encouragement, and more. The potential for growth through dream study is limitless. Whatever method or methods you use to gain a deeper understanding of your dreams, you are certain to discover the value of letting dream guidance be an important part of your spiritual journey.

---

*This five-step approach is an individualized adaptation of a group dream process developed by Montague Ullman, M.D., largely based on the material in the Edgar Cayce readings on dream interpretation. A version of this approach was first published in 1978 by the Association for Research and Enlightenment, Inc., in the home-study course, "Awakening the Dreamer."

4

Applying Past-Life Influences

REINCARNATION IS THE THEORY that, as souls, we each experience many lifetimes for the purpose of developing spiritually and becoming true cocreators with God. Some cultures and religious traditions teach the transmigration of souls; that is, that a soul can incarnate as human, animal, or even insect. However, in the model of reincarnation which Cayce embraced, the souls of humans, animals, and other creatures are totally different, with separate purposes and environments in which to seek perfection.

If this is an accurate interpretation of the human soul's

appearances in the earth, then, potentially, we have all experienced numerous lives throughout human history, through diverse cultures, within all races, as both male and female, in every type of economic, social, and political circumstance. We may have experienced every religious conviction, devoted ourselves to a life of service or to amassing material wealth, raised families, lived a celibate life, and fought, killed, or died for our convictions. We may have experienced peace in an idyllic setting, felt the thrill of adventure and discovery, developed a gift or talent, or all of these.

Cayce suggests that, from a spiritual perspective, we may both lose and gain in a given lifetime through the choices we make. For example, we may have at one time experienced a life of great power and vast wealth, a seemingly perfect existence. However, if we chose to use that power in a manner detrimental to others, we may have lost ground from a spiritual perspective. If we used our position of affluence to bring comfort to those less fortunate, we may have increased our spiritual understanding through the application of that compassion.

Ideally, the recognition of our soul's direct connection with our Creator is gradually enhanced and our spiritual development deepened through our lifetimes on earth. As we attempt to fulfill our unique purposes, we grow with each incarnation, adding depth and breadth to our many levels of understanding. This knowledge then becomes available to us through our intuition.

Two main components of reincarnation as described in the Cayce material are important to address, because they help us to understand this dynamic life cycle. These are *karma* and *grace*. In very basic terms, karma is the law of cause and effect: We reap what we sow, whether in this lifetime or in one to come. If we plant within ourselves seeds of resentment, hatred, intolerance, or harsh judgments through our thoughts, words, or actions, we eventually draw those things to us in one form or another.

> ... whatsoever an entity, an individual sows, that must he reap. That as law cannot be changed. As to whether one meets it in the letter of the law or in mercy, in grace, becomes the choice of the entity.
> 5001-1

So, if we are loving, gentle, kind, and caring in our thoughts and interactions with others, we will magnify those qualities in ourselves and see them reflected back to us in others. Regardless of the situations in which we find ourselves, how we act or react determines what we sow within ourselves.

Without an awareness of past-life experiences, we continue to act and react in what become karmic patterns. We might liken them to old television reruns—the plot never changes. The characters never develop. They are bound to replay endlessly the same missteps and routines.

We move out of the cycle of karma and into a state of grace when we consciously choose to change the pattern and act out of unconditional love rather than react as we previously have. We can choose to respond to difficult, even painful, experiences with love, compassion, and forgiveness. Jesus offered us the supreme example of grace in action when He cried out from the cross, "Father, forgive them, for they know not what they do."

Another aspect of reincarnation that is helpful in examining past-life influences is that we choose the parents and environment into which we are born. Now, it might appear that some of us are better at making those choices than others! But apparently that choice has to do with the larger picture of our soul growth; we incarnate into an experience that will allow us the opportunity to learn and grow in the ways in which we have need. Not that everything we experience is predestined; indeed, we all have the ability to exercise our free will and are sometimes at the mercy of others expressing theirs. But the ultimate responsibility for our spiritual growth rests within each one of us, from the choice to enter a life experience to every other choice we make in relationship to our ideal.

Cayce also suggested that souls tend to reincarnate in groups. Because of soul memory, we are drawn to people and circumstances that have been important influences in previous experiences. We have many traveling companions on this journey. For example, our co-workers of today might have been part of our monastery in another lifetime. Our current parents might have been our siblings or cousins previously. Close friends in this life might have been relatives in another. Though it may be difficult to understand at times, the ultimate purpose for our coming together again and again is to be teachers for one another as well as students on our spiritual journeys.

For, one enters a material sojourn not by chance, but there is brought into being the continuity of pattern or purpose, and each soul is attracted to those influences that may be visioned from above. Thus *there* the turns in the river of life may be viewed.

To be sure, there are floods in the life; there are dark days and there are days of sunshine. But the soul-entity stayed in a purpose that is creative, even as this entity, may find the haven of peace as is declared in [the Creator]. 3128-1

We might wonder why memories of these previous lifetimes are so inaccessible, especially if they can be helpful. The following quote from the Cayce readings seems to imply that the information becomes available to us only as it becomes pertinent or useful to our immediate circumstances; these memories surface from our own soul's memory banks as we have need of them.

> One may ask, as this entity—*why,* then, does one not recall more often those experiences?
>
> The same may be asked of why there is not the remembering of the time when two and two to the entity became four, or when C A T spelled cat. It always did! Ye only became aware of same as it became necessary for its practical application in the experience!
>
> So with the application of self's experience in material sojourns. When the necessity arises, as to how, where and in what direction those opportunities were applied, the entity brings those influences to bear in its relationships to daily problems. 2301-4

Benefits of Recognizing Past-Life Influences

The purpose of this chapter is to suggest methods for becoming conscious of past-life memories and to explain how to apply those insights in our present circumstances. When we learn to recognize those thoughts, feelings, actions, and reactions which result from past-life experiences, we can gain insights into our own nature, into our relationships with others, and even into our personal relationship with God.

We can choose how to act or react, just as we can choose which feelings to give energy to or those we would rather try to release. We can learn how to better focus our talents and abilities in order to express our true selves or to embark on a new career path. We can better understand which relationships need to be nurtured and which need to be healed. We can find ways to redirect negative behavior patterns or to forgive ourselves and others. What seemed impossible before we understood a past-life connection can suddenly seem natural, even easy. Sometimes, just recognizing past associations gives us enough emotional objectivity to release and move on. Emotions are our link across time from one life experience to the next. Carolyn Gelone, spiritual counselor, author, and former educator, explains the connection. "The emotional link is the tie that binds us to the memories of the past. According to the Cayce readings, emotions experienced on the earth plane are met again in later lives . . . They come to us in what Cayce called 'urges.' The emotional urges that are negative usually have a limiting aspect, and they affect growth patterns adversely."

Negative emotions or urges are those which we might need to transform in some way. When the urge is joyful or hopeful, we can take steps to express those positive memories or abilities in our current life circumstances. Not only can we find solutions to very tangible concerns through recognizing past-life memories, but, as with many other forms of intuitive insights, we also can make tremendous strides in healing relationships and promoting our own spiritual growth. As with all forms of intuitive knowledge, we need to access and apply that information with discernment and balance, with a genuine desire to learn, and, most important, with a firm commitment to following our unique spiritual path. When we do so, the potential for personal growth from the application of this knowledge is infinite.

Unlocking Clues to Past Lives

How do we know when a current situation is being influenced by a previous incarnation? Glimpses of past-life memories come to us in a variety of ways. By learning to recognize clues, we can bring that intuition more fully into consciousness. The following are examples of clues to past-life influences:

• *Instant, unexplainable recognition of a person you've never met or a place you've never been.* Holly related the following experience she had while on a trip through the English countryside:

"I was going to skip visiting this particular cathedral; we'd seen so many on the tour. But I decided to go through quickly anyway. Stepping into the sanctuary, I was overcome by a desire to bow down on the cold stone floor. I instead sat in a nearby pew for a few moments to get my bearings. Then I made my way to the choir loft at the front of the cathedral. Within moments, I could hear an invisible choir singing and recognized within the music my father's deep voice. Since he had recently passed away, I felt comforted; perhaps this was the experience for which I had been drawn in. As I exited the loft, I became aware that there was something else I needed to see. A priest approached and asked if everything was all right. I tried to explain my experience and he responded, 'This isn't the *only* church on this site, you know.' He then led me outside, down a stone stairway and through a huge wooden door into an ancient Norman chapel. At once, I knew the place—the round room with benches along the side, the round stone altar in the front, and the intricate arched design of the ceiling. All feelings of anxiety and discomfort dissipated, leaving me with a wonderful peaceful feeling."

• *Strong emotional reactions; unexplained fears, animosity toward someone, or, conversely, instant attraction and connection.* Carol Ann recounted a spontaneous past-life recollection in response to a puzzling emotional development in her relationship with her new husband.

"I had been wondering why I had such an emotional reaction whenever William would go out of town. I would be inexplicably clingy and tearful, afraid for his safety, and anxious that he wouldn't return. One morning, while discussing it together, I suddenly saw myself standing in the doorway of a prairie homestead, long skirt trailing around my ankles, waving good-bye as he rode off with the horse and wagon. He was going to St. Louis for supplies and was expected to be gone for several days. My next impression was several men bringing him back dead, and I started crying uncontrollably. I felt that it was accidental; apparently there had been a storm and a tree had fallen on him."

After the initial images, Carol Ann tried to retain the feeling of the experience in order to get a better sense of the time period and the nature of their relationship:

"I stayed with the vision and saw that we'd had two sons, and a third child was on the way. Our younger son was 'helping' William mend a fence, looking up at him with special admiration . . . In this lifetime, William is very handy at building things, and he seemed to have the same talent then . . . "

• *Unexplained talent or desire to pursue a particular profession or hobby.* From the above example, we might conclude that William's special knack for building things in this lifetime could be a talent he developed in his life on the prairie. In the following example, we see how extraordinary talent can manifest at a very young age.

Jean shared the story of her nephew, who at the age of five received a new basketball. Within moments of acquiring it, this young boy could dribble the ball expertly and shoot hoops with perfection. When asked how he had learned to play so well, he replied, "I used to practice all the time when I was a teenager."

Similarly, Mozart composed complex pieces of music as early as age five. This tremendous musical ability is nearly impossible to explain, except through the theory of reincarnation. Edgar Cayce himself was told in many of his personal life readings that he had been adept in the psychic and spiritual realms and had been a healer in a number of his previous lifetimes. Those gifts did not go away, but were enhanced and utilized in more creative ways than before.

- *A physical challenge or hardship that seems to have no basis in current reality.* Carolyn had always wanted to wear contact lenses, but, despite numerous attempts, she experienced severe eye irritations that made wearing contacts impossible. Doctors could find no physical reason for her discomfort. Carolyn decided to undergo a hypnotic past-life regression to recall a lifetime that might have triggered this strange physical reaction.

The appropriate memory came through with a gruesome but poignant image that left no doubt in her mind as to its relationship to her current condition. Carolyn saw herself in an ancient setting where she was being tortured. A startlingly graphic scene unfolded in which her eyes were poked out with wooden stakes! From that image she knew immediately why she was so fearful of putting foreign objects in her eyes in her present lifetime.

- *Accessing information without prior learning.* Nancy's niece Willa was only three years old when she began listening to operas and watching a videotape of Mozart's *The Magic Flute.* She seemed to have an uncanny ability to mimic the German dialogue from the tape, even though no one in her family spoke that language. Two years later, while Nancy was visiting, Willa began speaking in German. When asked why, Willa said, "Oh, I just get so tired of speaking English."

Willa's unusual ability and desire to listen to Mozart's music at such a young age might be a carry-over from a former lifetime in which she had some close connection with the composer.

- *Recognizing patterns in yourself that aren't apparent in other family members.* Erica described an experience that answered many perplexing questions:
"A friend and I went to visit The Cloisters museum, which was originally a monastery. We walked through rooms filled with tapestries, paintings, and other art. We admired the perfectly manicured, peaceful gardens. I especially enjoyed the piped-in Gregorian chants that filled the patios, though I had never before heard those sounds.

"Going back inside, I pushed open the huge oak door and glanced at the floor to be sure of my footing. What I saw when I looked down amazed me. Rather than my sneakers, I saw sandaled feet and, above that, a coarse brown robe. Just a flash and then it was gone.

"I told my friend, who had studied the Cayce material, about the experience. She just smiled and said, 'You've been there before.'

"The thought that I may once have been a monk helps to explain some aspects of myself. I have a quiet reserve that differs from my buoyant family. I am religious in that I have a conscientious approach to most things—consistent, mindful, and respectful. I adore lettering of all kinds and dabble with calligraphy. As a child, I enjoyed sitting alone and just being quiet. My whole view of life seemed very different from my family and schoolmates."

- *Spontaneous past-life recall in children.* One parent told us that three-year-old Timothy once declared, "I'm glad I'm a boy this time. I was a girl last time, and it was really boring!" A four-year-old boy, Martin, often talked of having flown planes before. Once while watching a television show in which a plane crashed, he burst into tears, crying that it was just like what happened to his beautiful plane. Martha shared an experience with her granddaughter, Peggy, who commented, "Remember when *I* was the mommy, and you were *my* little girl?"

Cayce suggested that parents write down statements and experiences such as these to share with their children at a future time. Children have much easier access to past-life experiences; those memories are closer to the surface and have not yet been screened out from their consciousness. However, these memories are as difficult to hold onto as the wisps of a dream and may quickly dissipate and be forgotten unless they are recorded.

Enhancing Sensitivity to Past-Life Influences

Answering the following questions can prompt an enhanced awareness of those past-life influences:

• To which countries and cultures do you feel an attraction or repulsion? What styles of furniture, architecture, clothing, and so on do you like? If the furnishings and accessories in your home or workplace reflect an interest in particular cultures, it is likely they are pertinent to a previous incarnation and are having an impact on your present circumstances.

• Do any nationalities or cultures come to mind when you meet a new person? If so, you both may be influenced by shared experiences from a previous lifetime. The dominant characteristics of that culture might give you clues about relating to that individual, based on remembered patterns and tendencies.

• What types of music, art, literature, and food do you most enjoy? Pursuing artistic endeavors is an excellent way to evoke past-life talents and memories.

• What patterns do you see in the hobbies and activities you choose? Are there pastimes you share with others? This is a good way to determine the nature of any past-life connections you may share.

In addition to reflecting on the above questions, if possible take some time to travel to locations that fascinate you or where you suspect you may have lived before. If you are unable to go there "literally," indulge in a bit of "virtual" travel by reading historical books or browsing the World Wide Web for sites pertaining to the countries that interest you. Also read everything you can find about a particular person, place, or event that you have found to be intriguing.

Ways of Working with Past-life Recall

Like many of the personal examples mentioned, we sometimes find ourselves in situations where our responses to people, situations, or even inanimate objects are confusing. It feels as though there is something significant going on, but we just can't put our finger on what. Rather than shrugging off such hunches, it can be helpful to seek further guidance and insight.

There are many avenues through which we can experience past-life recall. Some memories seem to come to us spontaneously. At other times, we can become aware of them by focusing on a particular puzzle and asking for insight from our higher selves.

It can become very tempting to get caught up in the mystery and challenge of delving into past lives, sometimes to the detriment of the current life experience. That is why we keep coming back to ideals, meditation, and prayer. What we are really suggesting is putting your spiritual life first and seeking insights that will be safe and practical. How you apply those insights in your daily experience will affect your spiritual growth.

Rob Grant shared an interesting bit of insight that he received firsthand from Hugh Lynn Cayce regarding recognizing past-life memories:

"When we spoke about past-life memories, Hugh Lynn suggested that I think back to my senior year in high school to a random event. He then told me to close my eyes and remember it. When I did, he asked, 'Do you see some scene?' I responded yes, that I was seeing a class picnic. 'OK, that's exactly the way past-life memories come back, the same way you remember this life,' he said. 'You sort of see it, but not completely. That's the way past-life images come to you.'"

Prayer and Meditation

Often, spiritually devoted individuals will experience spontaneous past-life recall while in a meditative state. One way of facilitating that type of recall is to hold in your mind as you enter into meditation a particular person or situation for which you have concern and ask for understanding.

One such flash happened to Giselle, a longtime meditator. She had been having some difficulties with a friend and co-worker, Alice, whose recent behavior she couldn't understand. They worked for a company whose employees frequently made presentations at large conferences. Giselle enjoyed this aspect of her work and was an excellent and well-respected speaker. Alice, who was in charge of organizing these functions, frequently overlooked Giselle when scheduling presenters. This exclusion from the roster seemed quite blatant, even coming to the attention of other employees. When Giselle broached the subject with Alice, she was given evasive answers. To Giselle, it seemed that Alice was holding something back, acting as though it were just an oversight. But, the "oversights" continued.

It was while contending with yet another omission that Giselle experienced her flash vision. As she was coming out of a deep meditative state, Giselle suddenly saw herself and Alice very vividly in a French theater setting during the late nineteenth century. She knew that they were both young ballerinas in that life as well as very good friends. There was one major problem between them, however. Giselle was the better dancer of the two and was regularly given the lead roles; Alice was jealous of her friend's preferential position and talent. When Alice died suddenly in the prime of her dancing career, she still harbored that resentment and jealousy. She also felt guilty for having these feelings, as Giselle had always been a loyal friend.

Giselle immediately understood the conflict with Alice, whose feelings remained unresolved. In her current position, Alice held some authority over Giselle and allowed those unconscious emotions to dominate. Her behavior prevented Giselle from successfully expressing her talents this time around. Having this memory flash did not make Giselle angry or resentful. Instead, because she truly loved her friend (in both lifetimes), she was able to be compassionate about the pain and anguish Alice still experienced in response to Giselle's success. She saw her friend as a vulnerable, hurt ballerina who was never able to openly process all of her emotions.

Giselle decided to deal with the issue in a more loving way, by praying for Alice daily and making an effort to sincerely compliment her work. The results of this approach were amazingly positive. Without another word about the issue, Alice began scheduling Giselle on the presentation roster. Their relationship improved dramatically after that experience.

Dreams

Dreams can provide spectacular glimpses of past lives, offering insights relevant to our current circumstances and relationships. Sometimes these dreams come as a result of a concern, or in response to a question posed in meditation. Because dreams are one of the most direct ways that our higher selves communicate with our conscious minds, we can ask for dreams that will help in understanding any aspect of our lives.

Rob shared a technique that he and a friend used to

incubate a dream about their friendship. "One of my closest friends in the navy was my roommate, Chet. We both joined a study group and began working regularly with our dreams. We kept daily dream journals and were following the guidance of a mentor, who suggested a technique for remembering past lives. He suggested we write down the words, 'Please show me in my dreams who I was in a past-life, for my better unfoldment.' Chet and I agreed to do this for thirty days, because we knew there was a deep connection between us and were curious to find out why. After the thirty days, we shared our journals and found two almost identical dreams of a lifetime in Greece. We had the dreams within a day or two of each other and were quite astonished . . . The dreams seemed to resonate with our friendship, and the Greek setting struck a chord for us both. Writing the phrase 'Please show me in my dreams . . . ' gave it a focus. It is like writing a letter to your subconscious mind—to your higher self. You can get information on anything in that manner; it's very effective."

Vanessa recounted a series of more than six dreams in which she saw herself with a man whom she had just met while on a trip to Egypt. She had not been consciously thinking about starting a new relationship with anyone, but the spontaneity and intensity with which these dreams occurred compelled her to consider them meaningful and worthy of exploration.

The content of these vivid dreams included detailed settings and clothing from distinct eras in Palestine, Egypt, France, and Africa. In them she was clearly shown that she and her new friend shared a special bond and that they had been involved in a variety of spiritual practices and forms of healing in many prior lifetimes. As a result of sharing and examining Vanessa's dreams together, their current relationship blossomed. They share a commitment to express creatively the spiritual insights and intuitive abilities garnered from those previous life-times as well as to develop and apply their present talents in service to others.

Body Work

There are many methods of applying touch to the body for the purpose of maintaining or promoting health. These techniques may facilitate physical and mental relaxation, increase blood flow, stimulate lymph circulation, or balance energy. It is possible, in the process of receiving these treatments, to gain insights into past-life experiences. Perhaps our higher selves are slipping them in when our minds and bodies are relaxed and open to guidance from within.

Justin became aware of a sudden past-life image while receiving a deep massage/shiatsu treatment. It was a very quick insight that was difficult for him to articulate, but evoked feelings that helped him understand the root of a long-term personality clash with his brother, Tom. He knew intuitively from the memory that he had left this younger brother behind during the big move west in early America, promising to send for him later. Unfortunately, he never succeeded financially and didn't have the means to bring Tom out to meet him.

Justin recognized the truth to this memory and finally understood why his brother responded to him with resentment and distrust. Because Tom was open to the concept of reincarnation, Justin shared the experience. The memory hit home with Tom as well and resulted in a dialogue between the two that brought about healing for them both.

Flashes of Knowing

Past-life memories can also come to us as flashes of understanding while in a conscious state of mind. At times, they come as instant familiarity with a person we just met or with someone we've known for years.

In an earlier example, Carol Ann shared her instant recall of a life on the prairie where her husband was killed accidentally. Carol Ann's memories were quite detailed and consistent with her husband's current personality traits as well as their shared lifestyle. The memories enabled her to gain a new perspective on her anxiety about William's business trips. Many times, just viewing the circumstances from another lifetime is enough to trigger positive changes, as resulted in Carol's case.

Sometimes, repetitious patterns or juxtapositions of people, objects, or events can trigger past-life memory recall. Doris experienced such a recall while she shared a pleasant summer's day with friends. There had always been an affinity within this group of seven, but for some reason their most enjoyable times together were in the hot summer months. Entire winters and springs could go by when they wouldn't see one another; but once summer hit, they were inseparable.

Doris had her flash just after a wonderful cookout and walk on the beach. The group was sitting in a circle outdoors with a candle glowing in the warmth of the sunset. As they listened to music, laughed, and simply enjoyed one another's company, Doris suddenly saw them all sitting around a campfire on a beach that she "knew" was in Polynesia in the distant past. The men wore only loincloth-type clothing, and the women little more than that. It was such a shocking experience that the others in the group asked Doris if she had just seen a ghost.

Doris tried to explain to the group what she had seen, much to their enjoyment. In retrospect, she felt that the flash of insight was a blessed gift—a beautiful, affirming memory come to life. They had all been drawn back together again in a spirit of love, camaraderie, and appreciation of life that transcended the boundaries of time.

Past-Life Regression

Past-life regression is a technique in which a trained practitioner uses hypnosis to gently guide the seeker to recall experiences from a previous incarnation. Carolyn Gelone uses past-life regressions in her work as a spiritual counselor. She explained the process as "an awareness technique that can help people deal with today's circumstances. It is a highly personal experience to be used when the person is truly ready to change something in his or her life."

The following example illustrates how we can gain a broader perspective on life and a greater understanding of our emotions and interpersonal dynamics through a past-life regression. This experience happened to Patricia, who had come to Carolyn for assistance. Patricia is a well-established doctor in a large city, the mother of five children, and was married to a man who is also a doctor. After many years of marriage, she realized the love had gone out of their relationship and that they were both frustrated and dissatisfied. In spite of that, Pat couldn't bring herself to suggest a divorce. She feared that if she left her husband she would be unable to survive, even though she was independently successful in her own medical practice. She decided a regression would help her understand the origin of her overwhelming fear of even discussing the issue with her husband.

In the session, Patricia saw herself in a lifetime in France as a beautiful, light-hearted, Parisian girl who married a much older, wealthy gentleman—her husband in this lifetime. After their marriage, he took her to live on his country estate where he would frequently leave her alone, isolated from the company and activity she was used to in Paris. Lonely and despondent, she begged him to move back to Paris. He refused to comply with her request and would not discuss it further.

As time passed, the vibrant young girl became a depressed, frustrated woman with no outlets for her energy, intelligence, or outgoing personality. In desperation, she ran away to Paris, hoping to start over in the city she loved. Tragically, her husband became outraged at her departure, discovered her whereabouts, and killed her. When this memory surfaced, Pat understood her inordinate fear of addressing the issue with her husband and her anxiety about surviving financially on her own. She worked to release those emotions and, after a few months, went to her husband and discussed a separation. He agreed peaceably to move nearby so that he could still see their children regularly. She worked through her fears, and everyone gained from the situation.

Travel

Hugh Lynn Cayce frequently advised people about the various ways they could develop their intuitive faculties and gain insights from certain activities. He suggested traveling as a method for increasing awareness of previous lifetimes. The break from the routine was invaluable in allowing prior memories to surface and for random insights to occur.

He emphasized that this was particularly meaningful when traveling to destinations with which you feel a particular resonance. In fact, Hugh Lynn's theory of triggering past-life understanding through travel was a primary reason for starting A.R.E.'s international tour program. These tours take participants to many of the locations described in the Cayce readings. They are well-balanced and spiritually focused, providing a holistic and intellectually challenging experience.

The following story illustrates how a combination of past-life regression and subsequent travel triggered a meaningful memory:

Marcus shared his amazement at the results of his first

group regression with hypnotist Henry Bolduc. Marcus clearly saw himself in an ancient Grecian theater and could literally feel himself being there. He knew without a doubt that he was involved with the theater, music, and the arts, and that his occupation back then was connected with the government. All of those areas are of great interest to him in his current lifetime; in fact, he works for the government!

Several months after that regression, Marcus had the opportunity to visit Greece. He found the experience re-affirming on all levels and enjoyed the chance to reconnect with those strong past-life memories. The emotional impact of that visit solidified his belief in reincarnation. It also demonstrated to him that we retain former talents and interests that we can continue to enhance and develop.

Déjà Vu: Indicator of Past-Life Memory

The following story provides an intriguing and complex illustration of many of the elements of past-life memories, influences, and inclinations which have been discussed throughout this chapter. It emphasizes the notion that the information becomes available as we have need of it and as we can apply it practically in our lives. Recognizing the source of strong emotional impulses and discovering relationships and karmic patterns that have traversed the limits of time are all part of this experience.

Lisette's experience spans ten years, from her first spontaneous insight to the reconciliation of deep emotional pain and release of limiting beliefs. It began as an intuitive flashback so emotionally charged that she decided to seek additional guidance through meditation, dreams, past-life regressions, and even a professional psychic. Over time, enough clues emerged that Lisette was able to formulate a clear message that she could apply to her life in helpful ways.

"I was sent to Hong Kong on business and during my free time decided to take a tour of an old Chinese village. It was after the village tour that some remarkable events occurred.

"As I wandered around the village on my own, I noticed a small pathway leading to a quaint little museum . . . It was dedicated to all the Chinese emperors from way back, depicting how they dressed in their respective eras and displaying all the accouterments that were important to each. They might be surrounded by replicas of whomever or whatever was significant to them, such as an image of their wife, a favorite animal, a concubine, the high priest, emblems and furnishings . . . One emperor's display piqued my interest especially, because his statue was sitting in Buddha fashion on the floor, very plainly, with nothing else around him—a real departure from the others. I was fascinated to read his descriptive plaque, which said that he was the only emperor who had decided not to allow China to be ruled by his only son, but rather by his prime minister, the man who most deserved to rule.

"The flash happened as I read the plaque and thought, 'Oh, yeah, that soul was also Jean Jacques Rousseau, the father of the French Revolution.' His philosophy was against the divine right of kings, and his writings were instrumental in prompting the whole mentality change that came about during that revolutionary era.

"The next thing I knew, as I looked over my right shoulder, I could see long, dirty brown hair flickering . . . I suddenly felt that it was my hair, my body, and I was very uncomfortable being so unclean . . . As I looked at the scene around me, I realized I was on a cart with hay at my feet . . . and instinctively knew that this was eighteenth-century France . . . I noticed people in the street around me whom I recognized as a part of my current lifetime.

"I was an aristocrat being paraded through the streets as an example to others. Although I wasn't guillotined, I was imprisoned for not giving in to the senseless accusations of the mob that arrested me. I felt totally alone and abandoned, because no one came to my aid—not my parents, not my husband, not even a friend. Abandonment is an issue I have wrestled with repeatedly in this current lifetime. My failure then to comply with what I perceived as the hypocritical demands of my accusers and refusal to maintain the status quo infuriated my husband. He refused to take me back when I was eventually released from prison. My parents felt it was unwise for me to stay in Paris with them, so they helped pay for me to go to England and ultimately to emigrate to post-Revolutionary America."

Lisette also explained that she always had a tremendous aversion toward anything French in this lifetime, but never understood why. Paradoxically, she was born to French parents in a part of New England where the French language predominated in daily life. She didn't even learn to speak English until she was four years old. After experiencing the memory of her former life in France, Lisette could finally understand why she had such negative emotions connected with it.

Her story has a happy ending on several counts. As a result of working with this past-life information, Lisette finally had a reckoning with the emotional and spiritual issues related to the French incarnation.

"While still processing these concerns, I was laid off from my job and subsequently hired by another large corporation. Ironically, the reason they hired me was because I could speak French. The company sent me to France, gave me refresher classes during the day, and treated me extremely well . . .

"During my stay in Paris, I experienced an apprehension about visiting the two islands in the middle of the city, particularly the Ile de la Cité. I discovered why, when I walked down a particular block and couldn't go a step farther. I asked my friend Linda to go ahead around the corner as I described to her exactly what she would see . . . It was La Conciergerie, the prison used during the French Revolution after the destruction of the Bastille."

Lisette was flooded with emotion as she looked at her former place of imprisonment, confirming the accuracy of the past-life memory with her own precise description of the entire compound and chapel.

As a result of these experiences, Lisette came to terms with her lifelong feeling of being inadequately nurtured by her parents. She explains: "I had just moved and, during my parents' first visit, came down with a terrible cold. When they arrived, I had so much congestion that laryngitis set in and I could barely talk. I told them it would be unfair to spend the day with them as we had planned, because I was so ill. Later that night, after being alone all day, I started to feel very uncared for because they didn't call to see how I felt. The next day, there was still no word from them. Finally, feeling very desolate and hurt, I slammed down the book I was reading and said, 'Look at this, nobody cares.' And all of a sudden I had a flashback to that feeling in France . . . and I said, 'Oh, my goodness, I re-created the exact same family situation to get this feeling.' I couldn't believe how vivid the realization of it was.

"The repetition of this experience allowed me to clearly see the deep psychological belief I held that nobody cared. And my karma with France seemed to be totally broken since that company treated me with such respect."

This encounter with a very pertinent past life had a transformational effect on Lisette's current life. She re-

lated what she felt were the most valuable lessons learned:
"I now have an understanding of karmic patterns. I had mistakenly thought that it meant I had done someone wrong and had to right it. Or that they had wronged me and had to right it. Suddenly I realized that what is meant by patterns is 'belief patterns.' I held the belief system that I hated everything French. The hatred of anything has no place in heaven . . . and I decided I wanted to release that emotion and the deep soul belief that nobody cared . . . Recognizing it for what it was . . . gave me my parents back. Now I understand that the role they played enabled me to recognize my pattern of feeling abandoned and brought about a sense of instant forgiveness . . . Breaking that awful belief . . . was a real gift."

Applying Past-Life Insights in Present-Day Circumstances

One way of understanding the spiritual work of integrating past-life information is a formula which Carolyn Gelone describes as "reveal, release, reprogram, result." Once the information has been revealed and accepted into our consciousness, we can discern changes we might choose to make. As we understand the need for transformation, we can reprogram our thoughts or emotions to bring about that change.

When we commit to a change in attitude, an increase in compassion, or a release from a limiting belief, we strengthen our endeavor on the spiritual path. It isn't enough to simply *remember* previous-life encounters— the *application* of the insights is crucial to creating a new, more positive outcome.

An important element to be aware of when applying past-life influences is the integration of the memory on a heart level. Having an intellectual understanding and trying to simply change one's thought patterns is not sufficient to bring about true healing. A heartfelt connection evokes a genuine release and change of emotion.

Sometimes the practical application happens immediately, with little effort on our part. It is as if the knowledge of a past-life influence creates a shift in our consciousness, a tremendous "Aha!" that heralds an immediate release from negative emotions or limiting thoughts. At other times, the information directs us to the next step in the process of our spiritual work. This is the reprogramming stage. It usually involves making the leap from mere learning to true understanding and incorporating that new knowledge into the fabric of our being, thus strengthening and supporting our spiritual growth.

Working intuitively with past-life memories can be extremely rewarding, but it can also be a painful process. It is wise to be prepared for learning things about ourselves that may not be glamorous or flattering to our egos. That is why desire and intention to grow spiritually are key to reaping the benefits of the beauty and grace inherent in reincarnation.

The following are suggestions for how you can work with the information gleaned from past-life examination (reprogramming) to help bring about a transformation (result). Remember that changes can come about simply as a result of the desire for change, or they might require consistent, persistent attention over time. And, as with all spiritual and personal growth, the only person we can truly change is ourself.

- *Pray for the situation or person.*   Earlier we shared how Giselle was able to pray for Alice, once she understood their past-life connection as ballerinas. By turning the issue over to God, Giselle released her own negative responses, thereby stepping off the emotional treadmill she had been on. As a result, the situation improved dramatically.

- *Develop an affirmation to change a thought or belief pattern.* Because past-life memories are a combination of emotions and thoughts, when we choose to change one aspect, it can positively affect another. Affirmations should be stated in positive terms and can be repeated before meditation or at bedtime. Cayce indicated that using affirmations just before sleep would plant a seed in the unconscious, thereby helping to create positive change in the waking state. He called these affirmations "presleep suggestions."

Earlier in this chapter, we related Carolyn's experience of wanting to wear contact lenses but finding that her eyes were too sensitive. In a regression to gain insight into this difficulty, Carolyn "saw" herself being tortured by having her eyes poked out. Recognizing the deep-seated cause of her condition compelled Carolyn to reprogram her thinking and release her fearful habit patterns. She began a process of prayer and self-hypnosis in which she repeated positive affirmations prior to meditation and in a presleep state as well. The words of the affirmations told her body that everything was all right and that her eyes would be fine if contacts were placed in them. After several weeks of conscientiously applying this routine, Carolyn was able to wear contact lenses with ease.

- *Make a conscious change in your actions or perceptions.* Sometimes choosing to act or respond differently is all we need to do to create positive change. By engaging our free will, which Cayce called the "motivating force of the soul," we can release ourselves from karmic patterns and inertia and put that energy into motion, rather than remaining trapped in a holding pattern.

- *Find ways to bring into this life positive aspects from previous-life experiences.* As we discover the treasures we've gained in past experiences, we can choose to bring them into our conscious awareness. These treasures might include any of our creative talents or inclinations—a love of the outdoors, the ability to harmonize with others, a sense of adventure, and so on. By drawing on these evolving elements of who we are, we can strengthen our understanding of and connection to our higher selves and, ultimately, to God.

Excerpts of a Life Reading from Edgar Cayce

The following life reading was given to a thirty-three-year-old man on April 27, 1943. It examines the events of several past lives, then illustrates the influence of those experiences on present inclinations, interests, and talents. Cayce suggests to the recipient that he seek out the knowledge he gained in previous experiences and use it to understand his personal relationship with the universal forces:

Before this the entity was in the land of the present nativity, during the early settlings . . . on the island off the coast of Carolina . . .

The entity then in its activities became closely associated with the medicine men of those periods, and was acquainted with . . . one Powhatan . . .

Hence the entity's interest in healing, in the outdoors, in music . . . These abilities are manifested in the present in varied ways or manners . . .

Before that (there were others, but this we will give) the entity was in the Holy Land. We give this because it presents the urge that comes from those activities, in the abilities for detail work.

There the entity was in those groups that were not wholly of the Roman, not wholly of the Palestine land, and yet . . . working with both factions— which caused some confusion.

Yet the entity in that experience gained much. For the entity then was a bridge builder, as might be termed today, or a pioneer in the ways and means for transportation . . . being among the first in that particular period to build with timber.

Thus wood, types of wood have a particular interest; those things having to do with physics, and building—as engineering and activities of such natures . . .

In that experience, judged from man's judgment, the entity was a material success. Judged by his own experience, of not being satisfied—a failure—though the entity gained much through that period . . .

Before that the entity was in the Persian and Arabian land . . . For, the entity conducted a caravan that journeyed from the land of the hills, or from India, to Egypt—and passed through that area of the "city in the hills and the plains."

Thus the trades, the promptings and urges in individuals for adornment, as well as amusement, arise from those applications of the entity's abilities through that particular sojourn . . .

The entity gained throughout that period. For, the entity eventually established in the "city in the hills" a center, or a trading post, where those influences from the teacher Uhjltd brought an unfoldment to the entity—the consciousness that what is the better for all is the better for the individual, or the universal consciousness . . .

Then, in attaining . . . the outlet for thy abilities:

Choose that most in keeping with thy purposes, thy aims, thy desires. Are thy desires and thy purposes ideal, in thine own consciousness? What is thy ideal, spiritually? . . .

Thus may ye come to know thyself and thy rela-

tionship to thy Creative Forces . . . the manner in which ye treat thy brother is the manner in which thy growth is attained. As a merchant, as a tradesman, or as the engineer, ye may find the outlet for thy greater abilities.
2981-1

Conclusion

The focus of this chapter has been on recognizing and understanding the influence of past-life experiences in our current-life circumstances. But the real essence of the message is that we can use this understanding to make our lives better, more joyous, more whole, and less encumbered by unnoticed or misunderstood belief patterns. Ultimately, once we've used a little detective work to better understand our inner selves, we free up our energy to be of greater service to others. By allowing this information to come into our consciousness, and then using it in positive ways, we draw closer to those with whom we share our present earthly sojourn, and to the Source of Life itself.

5

Ordinary People–
Extraordinary Guidance

Every entity has clairvoyant, mystic, psychic powers . . . The intuitional, which is both clairvoyant *and* psychic, is the higher development . . . 1500-4

TAKE A MOMENT TO ask yourself this question: "How often do I go through the day feeling that nothing particularly insightful has happened or that the universe has allotted me a rather scant supply of psychic perception?" If your answer to this question is, "Quite often," then your perception of your own talents and what has taken place in the past twenty-four hours is self-limiting. A larger, universal perspective gives us a broader view of what is actually taking place in the conscious life we're leading and what our capacity for changing the ordinary into the extraordinary can ultimately be.

After speaking with dozens of presumably "nonpsychic" individuals, we have come to the conclusion that most people's lives are much richer and more intuitively based than they imagine.

> Know that the soul, the psychic forces of an entity, any entity, any body, are as eternal as that promise—for they are without days, without years, without numbers, but the *will* of man may make all at naught. For how *can* [we] be free unless will is a part of that Whole?
>
> Thus, making the will one with [the Creator], to be directed and guided by [the Creator], you shall know the truth and the truth shall make you free— you—You—*You!* 1376-1

This Cayce reading encourages each of us to take heed of our own power to discover insights from the world around us. By expressing and attuning our will with the Higher Will, we can discover our *personal truth*, thereby allowing ourselves to reunite with the Whole. We accomplish this, in part, by using our intuition more freely on a regular basis.

Intuitive Strengths

As we mentioned earlier, intuition manifests differently for each person. As we become aware of our particular intuitive strengths, we can increase our understanding and application of those insights. The examples from the Edgar Cayce readings which follow give us a sense of the variety of those experiences:

> By the mere mention of an incident or fact, the entity in the present the more often sees the end of same without knowing just how, where, or being

able to give any definite details. But more *often* it is correct. Intuition. 255-12

This is one individual . . . who may take long chances and win . . .
For the urges are such that when others sleep, or think the entity sleeps, the mind works and he has the answer to the other fellow's problem and can beat him at his own game. 5163-1

. . . the body itself has a great deal of intuition or insight as to what, who, how individuals fit into the various conditions or various fields that may be covered . . . and there will come *to* the body that necessary for the undertaking. 658-13

Perhaps it is easiest to follow the example of young children when pursuing intuitive growth, watching how their behavior often expresses these capabilities in the most unhampered and innocent manner. Children seem to maintain a natural connection with the spiritual realms and are (thankfully) too uninhibited to censor their insights.

It is quite common for parents to experience an intuitive bond with their children, which reinforces the idea that feeling love toward someone and making a heart-centered connection with him or her seems to strengthen the frequency and/or accuracy of intuitive insights gained about that individual.

Helen demonstrated telepathic abilities regularly. One particularly noteworthy instance occurred when, at the age of eight, she began to speak some words in a foreign language of which she had no prior knowledge. Both her parents practiced martial arts and utilized Japanese in their training. On this occasion, the family was eating in relative silence. Earlier in the evening, their training session had focused upon a particular form with a distinctive Japanese name, and both parents were reviewing the movements in their minds. Neither had mentioned anything about it to their children, and they were unaware that they were both thinking of it simultaneously. The silence in the room was suddenly broken as Helen blurted out the name of the specific kata, or training form, clear as a bell with the correct Japanese pronunciation.

This startling experience clearly demonstrated Helen's openness to and awareness of thought levels beyond the audible, physical realm. But, more important, it displayed how closely attuned she was at that moment to the energy and consciousness of her parents. As an adult, she continues to maintain an unusually loving, intuitive relationship with both her parents and is still very telepathic.

The next story is more tragic in nature but illustrates the profound strength of a heartfelt connection between a mother and child and its sobering impact.

Therese told us of two experiences that occurred with her son, Jim. One took place when he was a baby, and the other, when he was seven years old.

"From the time Jim was just an infant, I felt an exceptionally strong bond with him. So strong, in fact, that whenever I would wake up in the morning—no matter if it was six o'clock or nine o'clock—the instant I opened my eyes, he would immediately begin to cry in the next room. We seemed to be bonded somehow on a psychic level."

Therese recalled a particularly dramatic event when Jim was about nine months old. "There was a connecting door between my bedroom and his which was open that night. I was in a deep, sound sleep . . . With my ever-listening mother's ear, I heard him make a very slight cough . . . and, for whatever reason, the next thing I knew

I was leaping out of bed, still half-asleep—he wasn't choking or anything, but . . . there I was, bounding into his room for no apparent reason, with his father leaping out right behind me. By the time we reached his room, Jim was already turning blue; so I hit him on the back and he started breathing again. I'm assuming it would have been like sudden infant death syndrome. To this day, I don't know what made me rush in there, but I really believe it saved his life."

Another incident took place about six years later when Jim's father, Ken, was planning to take his son out on a fishing trip. Ken, a commercial fisherman, was going to wake Jim up at four in the morning to get an early start. Therese knew this before she went to sleep. She described what took place. "I heard the alarm go off and was half-asleep as Ken went into the bathroom. Then I heard him go into Jim's room to wake him up. And as he began to do that, I suddenly heard a frightening voice inside my mind that screamed really, really loudly, 'No!' It was just the one word, and it felt as if that word filled my whole being. It was overwhelming, but I started talking myself out of being worried by it. I began saying, 'No?' 'Why would you say no?' 'Why can't he go?' 'What's he going to do, stay home and watch cartoons all day?' Those thoughts went through my head . . . but I finally quieted down and let him go with his father."

Therese spent the day running errands while they were fishing, and she had just put the house key in the front door lock when she heard the phone ringing. Sadly, the news she was told gave meaning to the horrible "No" she had heard in her head earlier in the morning. There had been a terrible accident, and Jim was in the hospital.

"He was in a motorboat and got thrown into the water. Because Jim was wearing a life preserver, he popped back up to the surface after being thrown overboard. But, unfortunately, he popped up directly under the propeller of the boat and lost his arm as a result."

We asked Therese how she felt after the accident in light of the voice she had heard in the morning. "Guilty," she replied. "I felt like . . . if I had only listened to myself, it might never have happened . . . Ever since then I haven't had an experience that was quite so dramatic, but whenever I get a strong intuitive sense not to do something or that I should do something, I try to follow it. It's never been through an audible voice like that again."

Heart Connections: Magnetic Reunions

Quite often, the loving connections we share among family members or friends can bring about what might be called *magnetic reunions.* A perfect example of this took place during summer vacation several years ago when Jessica and her best friend, Dorian, were about to enter their senior year in college.

Dorian had just finished a semester of study in France when Jessica and two friends were embarking on a three-week trek through five European countries. Because Dorian and her boyfriend had left France just prior to Jessica's visit, they were unable to connect by phone to share their respective itineraries.

Both young women were terribly disappointed by not knowing each other's whereabouts, so their moods were somewhat dampened. Yet each of their trips proceeded pleasantly.

Toward the end of her trip, Jessica and two friends stopped in a remote village in Switzerland. As they looked at some crafts on a quaint street corner, Jessica was startled to hear someone down the block calling her name. Looking up, she was thrilled to discover it was her much loved comrade, Dorian. They had their European rendezvous after all! It seemed to come about from the sheer power of their bond to one another. The energy of their desire to meet brought it about in a most unlikely spot.

Lessons in Heeding Your Own Insights

Ellen shared a story that involves a gut feeling or sense of knowing that would have been wise to follow, even at the risk of feeling foolish.

"While on a vacation trip to Boston, my traveling companion and I had several hours to spare before meeting a friend for dinner. We decided to visit the New England Aquarium in the meantime. As we drove toward a nearby parking garage, I felt somewhat uneasy, not sure that I should park my car there. I fussed at myself, convincing myself that I was just anxious about being in the city and that everything would be all right. When I pulled in, the anxious feeling turned to panic, and I decided to back up. Unfortunately, the entrance was equipped with a grate that slashed the tires of any vehicle attempting to back out. When I realized that I would have to drive through to the exit booth, I felt silly about explaining to the attendant that we decided not to park there. So, I again talked myself out of the uncomfortable feelings . . . left the car in the lot, and headed to the aquarium.

"Upon our return several hours later, we found that my car had been broken into and all our baggage stolen. The officer at the police station in sight of the parking garage was sympathetic, but was not surprised when I told him where we had parked . . . our plight was apparently a common occurrence at that location."

If she had only listened to her inner feelings, Ellen's vacation would have ended on a happier note and been memorable for a reason other than stolen luggage.

Practical Guidance from
Altered Levels of Awareness

Many encounters with other levels of consciousness—voices, visions, symbols from beyond—come to
us in ways and at the times we least expect and can be
vital tools for coping with the demands of daily living.
The first example below, experienced by Nancy from
ages nine to eleven, is similar to what Edgar Cayce experienced as a young boy, when he was able to recite his
entire spelling book verbatim after sleeping on it for several minutes.

"The experience of visually remembering was one I
had often, but never told anyone about. I referred to it as
my 'remembering time' and used this method (although
I never called it a method) whenever I did my homework.
It was a routine I followed regularly whenever I studied a
subject I liked, and it worked especially well with spelling and history.

"What I did, in retrospect, was put myself into a meditative state before I read the material. I called it 'being
quiet,' and I would always pray before I did it. This process entailed sitting on my bed, taking deep breaths, re-
laxing for a brief period in silence, and then focusing on
my studies for that night. I would look closely at the visual images on whatever pages I was reading and remember the position of the words and pictures. It didn't
take any effort to remember—it would just happen. But
I think it was different than just a photographic memory,
because I would first have a very strong 'feeling' about
the information I had just read. For instance, if I were
reading about Italy in the Middle Ages, I would somehow get a sense of what that was like. I let the words in
the book guide me. Thinking back on it now, I was probably utilizing past-life recall to bolster my understanding of the time period, culture, and so forth. After the

process was complete, I wouldn't think about it again until the teacher addressed the topic in class.

"Usually, when questions were asked about the specific chapter, I could literally see the answers to the questions next to the corresponding pictures on the page. All I had to do was put myself back into that same relaxed state, squint my eyes a little bit, and then 'feel' the image as it came into my mind. The process served me very well for a number of years, but, for whatever reason, it faded as time went on.

"I did, however, retain into adulthood the ability to remember things that I find of interest—usually things having to do with people. It seems to be one of the ways I am intuitive. I remember details about individuals that give me insight into their essence and greater understanding of their circumstances and emotional issues. This allows me to be of service to them. And it probably gave me a head start when I began meditating in earnest.

The following circumstances convey how a change in awareness turned Susan's traumatic sadness over the loss of a loved one into a life-transforming experience.

Susan shared her belief with us that the death of her brother, Gary, triggered her experience of "a place of peace and beauty" that she says "turned my sorrow into a new understanding of love."

"The night I heard my brother had died, I went into a kind of shock . . . I still recall the wail that started from somewhere deep inside me and ripped through my heart, escaping like a siren . . . in the word 'No!' 'No!' I tried . . . to gain some control, barely able to hear my father's . . . explanation through the telephone . . . sounding an eternity away.

"I would not have imagined in a thousand years that I'd react so uncontrollably to such news. After all, I'd been praying and meditating for years. I knew that life does not end with physical death. There had even been times when I would wonder what my reaction to the death of a loved one would be, and I'd always pictured myself calm and serene in the faith that life goes on. Yet when grief came for me, it left no mercy."

Susan's brother had experienced a massive heart attack at the early age of forty-eight. She traveled to Florida to her parents' home and went into the room where her brother had last stayed during his visit there.

"Sitting down on the bed where he had napped, I thought about his last moments.

"Gary had come over to my father's for a fishing trip. His wife later told me that Gary had said 'no' when my father originally invited him, because fishing always made him terribly seasick. He changed his mind after he thought about the fact that my father had been ill. He told her, 'We never know; this could be the last time I get to spend with him.' When the fishing trip was finished and they had returned home, Gary lay down to recuperate. A short while later, he came out of the room with severe chest pains."

Susan cried as she wondered about her brother's last moments of life and she audibly called out to him, "Gary, why?!" Her story continued, " . . . then as . . . if he were standing there in the flesh, I heard him say: 'Hey, Sue. It's OK. I'm at peace; now you go and be at peace. By the way, you were right.' And he was gone."

Although she continued to mourn her brother's passing, Susan began to feel a deep sense of peace during the remaining week. She definitely felt that something miraculous had taken place when she heard Gary's voice; but it wasn't until she began her long drive home alone that, as she puts it, a "new world" opened up for her.

As she drove down the road, Susan thought of her brother. "Softly weeping, I started wondering about his death and thought, 'Why?' As mysteriously as it had happened before, there was Gary's voice, but this time he explained. His answer was so clear and made such sense that I began asking more. One by one, he answered each question. Soon into this thirteen-hour session, the answers to my questions began coming from someone, some others, besides Gary. Perhaps it was because the nature of the questions had changed from personal to more universal: 'What is life all about?' 'Why are we here?' etc. It was as though Gary gave the floor to others more experienced.

"The best way I can describe this exchange is that the answers were not told to me, but, more accurately, shown . . . I no sooner thought the . . . question than the 'answer' returned to me. In between each one, I basked in the serenity and pervasive love that came with the information. This went on for the entire drive. By the time I arrived home, it was late. I fell asleep with an awareness of how . . . this experience had profoundly changed me.

"That night, I awoke . . . at about two o'clock and followed the urge to go downstairs to meditate. I . . . settled in for what was to be the deepest meditation . . . I have ever experienced. Again, I found myself in the presence of my brother, and behind him, these other beings. This time, in addition to hearing . . . I also saw and felt the [communication] as well.

"What I saw on the other side was literally breathtaking. The entities—exquisite focal points of light and energy—[were like] nothing on earth . . . The beings did not have bodies as we know them . . . I felt they were angels because they had . . . profound power and beauty . . . There were about five of them . . . I also was aware of otherworldly music."

Susan described how the question-and-answer sessions began once again. "The . . . answers paled in comparison to the feeling they shared with me of the connectedness of all souls, the understanding of the depth of this bond being far more important than any fact I could ever be given . . . They showed me that this energy and light emanating from them is the same as that which [connects] all of creation . . . people, animals . . . earth, the heavens . . . and me! . . . these beautiful beings helped me experience how, only to the level that we truly love ourselves, can we love anyone else . . . I understood for the first time what it means to be 'at one.'"

While feeling a profound sense of joy, Susan tells how she was led by the beings to an understanding of eternal life. And, as she explains it: "I saw the purpose of the flesh, how quickly our time in it passes, and how wonderful it feels to return home when our job on earth is finished. A peacefulness washed over me . . . knowing that these beautiful beings do indeed work with us and watch over us with a love that goes beyond human description."

Susan's regular communications with her brother and the special beings continued at the same time each night for several weeks until, eventually, the frequency lessened and the visits stopped altogether. She tried to meditate as she had always done, but became depressed in the absence of the exhilaration generated by her brother and the angelic beings. It was during this time of her feeling alone and depressed that she cried out, "Why have you left me?" The beings responded that she had become too dependent on them and that she needed to pray and meditate with the recognition that God is her Source, not them.

After going through a long period of isolation and sadness, Susan attended an A.R.E. conference entitled "We Don't Die." It was during a lecture by Dannion Brinkley, a man who had died and returned to life after twenty-eight minutes, that Susan finally felt a sense of resonance and release of the loneliness she had been feeling. She described how this event was a culminating experience for her, one she desperately needed at that time.

"Although I had not seen . . . a tunnel with bright light at the end of it . . . nor had I gained psychic abilities as [Dannion Brinkley] had . . . the essence of what he . . . spoke about was exactly like what had been shown to me . . . He also said something that struck a chord with me . . . He said the reason we are unable to recall the other side is because if we could, we would be too tempted to quit our time here on earth and, with our jobs incomplete, go back to the other side. Then I knew! The incredible loneliness I had been feeling was . . . homesickness. Not that I wanted my life here to end. I know I still have work to do, and I love my family and friends . . . But I was given a glimpse of "home" and had been longing for it. Understanding the feeling . . . released me from its grasp, and I was freed to get on with life, more joyously than ever before."

Since then, Susan has experienced a number of reassuring incidents that renewed her appreciation for the unconditional love we all share and her assurance that life is eternal. She has found numerous ways to apply this wonderful knowledge in her daily life for the benefit of others.

Warnings and Insights

Sometimes intuitive promptings seem aimed at helping us cope with inevitable situations; other times they seem designed to alert us to redirect our energy or change where we're headed. The following are examples of how ordinary people found themselves in *extra*ordinary states of awareness. The first came from Ellen:

"My friend Lisa had a rare form of cancer, which appeared in her right arm and grew quickly. After an operation in which the tumor and several lymph nodes in her right side were removed, Lisa seemed to be recovering. While visiting one fall day, Lisa was anxious to show me how well she was getting along. We went to her weight room, where she picked up a weight and started to work that arm. She asked me to come closer so that I could see what she was able to do. As soon as I got within her aura, a wave of fear and alarm swept over me, and I had to step back. In that instant, I knew that the cancer was even then silently attacking her body. Her next set of tests showed that the cancer had spread to her liver. She passed away the following spring."

In this instance, Ellen felt that she was being called upon to pray for her friend and that perhaps that prayer helped to ease Lisa's passing in some way.

Nancy told of a brief insight and firm but gentle warning she had while pregnant with her second child:

"Back in the early 1970s we weren't generally informed about the gender of our expected baby unless there was some health concern at issue. So, I had no idea what the sex of my second child might be. I was five months along in the pregnancy, and, although I knew it was probably not a good idea that far into the pregnancy, I began jumping rope. I was used to a lot of physical activity normally and was feeling particularly eager to have some strenuous exercise. Luckily, I got very sound advice from the baby in my womb. After just a half a minute or so, I literally heard the baby tell me to stop—and it let me know that I should expect a girl. It was so explicit and undeniable a message to me that I literally stood there for several minutes repeating gleefully, 'You're a girl! You're a little girl!! I'm sorry I was jumping rope. I'll stop now.'" And indeed, Nancy had a baby girl!

Conclusion

These examples of ordinary individuals having extraordinary guidance are representative of the tremendous capacity we have within us to attune to various levels of consciousness and to take advantage of a heightened level of awareness that is present around and within each of us every day. As humans on the exciting road leading into the future, we should take to heart these words of Paramahansa Yogananda and begin to apply our potential with joy, discernment, and true, unconditional love:

"Intuition is the discriminative faculty that enables you to decide which of two lines of reasoning is right. Perfect intuition makes you a master of all knowledge. Your will and intuition should go hand in hand. A person with a strong will usually has an active intuitional power. You should develop the latent intuitive faculty; it can grow only through meditation. Do not make unimportant things important, nor concentrate on trifles at the expense of vital matters, or you will hamper your progress. Impulsive actions that are not in keeping with one's real duties are undesirable. Let soul intuition guide your thinking, and then proceed confidently in any undertaking."

6

Professional Intuitives: How They Discern Guidance

If the body will then listen oft to that within, the directions may be more in keeping with that which will be satisfying or gratifying, and constructive in the experience. 1486-2

THERE IS A GREAT deal of interest these days in gaining information—about the past and present, but especially about the future. We all seem to want to know what is in store for us in the next few days, months, or years. Will my career be successful? When will I find the perfect companion? How should I invest my money? Where is the best place for me to live? The questions are endless, and most people seem willing to go to great lengths to find the answers, as evidenced by the tremendous increase in interest in psychic readings.

Edgar Cayce often admonished his clients to follow

their own guidance and to listen to the answers that they already had in hand for self's betterment. At the same time, he never turned away a person who was truly in need. The very nature of his life's calling as an intuitive counselor confirms the reality that there will always be circumstances in the life of every human being when outside advice or assistance will be needed.

It was true in Mr. Cayce's time, and it is still true today. What many people seeking the guidance of psychics frequently fail to remember, however, is that we must use balance and discernment when applying insights from other sources and that the sole responsibility for decisions based upon those insights lies with us. Psychic readings can only be used as tools or spiritual road maps to help us on our paths; they are not black-and-white answers to solving our life's riddles.

With that said, it is still reassuring to know that there are some of us who are much better at sensing psychic information than others, and the input of such intuitives can sometimes be of great service in helping us improve our lives.

In pursuing psychic realms of growth, the Edgar Cayce readings admonish that we should always consider the potential dangers and complications of intuitive development. Remaining true to our ideal is crucial to assuring that our path remains clear. Being aware of this balance is a necessary ingredient for any true seeker. This aspect is probably addressed less often, perhaps because it is the dark side of spiritual enlightenment. It can be viewed in the same category as St. John's "dark night of the soul," the place where fears vie for our attention and can keep us from ever progressing to the next level of understanding.

An appropriate and clarifying story from mythology was shared with us by Henry Reed, Ph.D., noted author, psychologist, and pioneer in the study of dreams and intuition. Henry has spent many years working with professional psychics and researching the ways their abilities develop. One overriding factor he has observed is the necessity for the intuitive to remain grounded and directed by the spiritual ideal in order to take full advantage of the higher realms of consciousness in a safe but open manner.

"There is a great lesson about this in the *Odyssey*," Henry said, "where Odysseus wants to sail his boat past the sirens, who are these female, goddesslike creatures that had these incredible songs and could send their listeners into ecstasy just by hearing their music. Odysseus wanted to experience that ecstasy, but the trouble was that if he did so, his ship would crash on the rocks as he entered the ecstatic state. This is the problem he faced and that many psychics face: How do you open yourself up to all this wonderful insight without crashing? So what's his solution? Well, he plugs up the ears of his crew members so they can't hear the music while they navigate the boat. He ties himself, who can hear, to the mast of the ship to prevent himself from doing anything weird. And then he orders his men to sail close by the sirens. Now, they can't hear it so they won't wreck the boat, but he can hear it and is tied to the mast of the ship, so he can go into ecstasy safely.

"If you look at this symbolically, the mast of the ship is really like the ideal. It is what some traditions would call the Tree of Life. It's the Oneness principle. It's the point to which we're going to attach our focus and use as our foundation, our anchor. So Odysseus anchors himself to that [ideal], and he can't get away from it. But he doesn't allow the lower self, represented by the crew members, to have access to this special experience. So their lower natures aren't aroused. Going all the way back in history, we have Homer to thank for this story that gives us a suggestion of how to work with these other realms and still stay within the positive aspects of it."

In learning any skill or discipline, it is always beneficial to examine the abilities of experts in a given field. So, in order to understand more about our own intuitive capabilities, it will help to hear how those insights come to professional psychics. This chapter focuses on a series of interviews with professional intuitives whose modalities of discernment are quite diverse. The next chapter offers input from professionals in various other creative fields who frequently receive intuitive guidance while performing or as a result of their particular occupations.

Truth in the Stars: An Astrologer's View of Intuition

In giving then the astrological aspects—these become as the innate or the intuitive influences, and naturally there is a great deal of the intuitive forces within the entity's experience. 1744-1

When we asked noted astrologer George Tripodi if he remembered the first time he experienced intuition coming through his astrology readings, he said he didn't. What he does remember, however, is his longtime attraction to the art of astrology. He and numerous other intuitives with whom we spoke indicated their sense of strong connection between doing what one loves and the ability to access psychic information. There seems to be a resonance factor that helps open up the flow of energy from the Higher Self (or Creative Forces) to the individual consciousness of the intuitive seeking the guidance. That connection is what enables the person to act as a conduit through which psychic information can flow.

George feels that somehow he is able to align himself with a person's soul energy and then look more deeply into life patterns by examining an astrological chart. He cannot articulate exactly how he is able to connect with the other person so effectively, except that he feels it is one of his innate abilities to have a strong sense of who a person is beyond the surface. Undoubtedly, that ability was strengthened by his previous profession as an executive placement consultant for various corporations. It is a process that has evolved considerably over time and continues to be a learning experience for George, as well as for his clients.

Back when he first started reading horoscopes for his family and friends, George had no intention of becoming a professional astrologer. But eventually, the demand became so great, as the inner truth and positive results of his astrological advice proved his ability, that he finally gave up his regular job to do astrology full time.

When he begins giving a reading, he said, a voice comes to him and his speech changes somewhat. The source of the information that comes through him, George believes, is his own higher self and/or the higher self of the client—both coming under the umbrella of a greater, universal force from which all of our creative energy and insights emanate. His astrology serves as a funneling tool that brings the material into a practical, everyday framework that is meaningful and beneficial to the recipient of the reading.

He doesn't allow himself to hold onto the advice he gives, and he conscientiously endeavors to release any ego-driven desire to control the outcome. It is also crucial, George believes, to impress upon the client how essential it is for the client to claim responsibility for decisions made as a result of the insights George shares. He explained:

"What I am doing really, as I start to interpret this information for individuals, is that I am asking them this question: *How will you manage your energy?*"

Since what he sees in the birth chart is essentially patterns of energy, George is simply presenting to the client the various directions in which that energy might be headed and what some of the options might be.

"It's all their decision, as I see it. I describe patterns from the past and possibilities for the future, and it is then up to the individual to determine how to work with the material."

There are certain common areas of guidance found in everyone's chart and elements that are specific to each individual. George first sees a soul's primary purpose in the horoscope. An example of this would be "the need to learn fairness and balance in life."

The secondary lesson that he extrapolates from the planetary aspects in a chart has more to do with the person's self-judgments and subjective view of the purpose for coming into the earth plane at this time. He describes it as "the way we perceive things to be in conflict in our personal lives—what we have decided to work on individually. It's a self-inflicted choice we've already made before or at the time of our birth."

Certain characteristics are shared by people born in a particular sign or under the influence of the same elements—earth, air, fire, or water—and he notes that the different elements seem to have an impact on how we process intuitive insights. In his experience, they generally break down into the following categories: Water signs (Pisces, Cancer, Scorpio) tend to internalize psychic information, feeling it first on an inner level and then letting it manifest in a feeling way; air signs (Aquarius, Gemini, Libra) are prone to intellectualize their intuitive insight, expressing it through mental, abstract means; earth signs (Capricorn, Taurus, Virgo) look at intuition from a very practical perspective and try to apply it in a material manner; and fire signs (Aries, Leo, Sagittarius) view intuitive insights from an idealistic standpoint and convey their impressions with inspiration, trying to live out the higher ideal.

In his years of reading countless charts, however, George has found one common quality that nearly everyone shares; that is, we are extremely self-judgmental. Most people find it difficult to love themselves truly and to recognize what George calls "their own God-ness." Until we accept that divine part of our nature, all the psychic readings in the world won't help us evoke and express our magnificent potential.

In conjunction with his own application of intuition, George sees the necessity for our society to head in a new and challenging direction as we enter the new millennium. He feels there are a number of people on the planet at this time who have an increased tolerance of fear. Those people are able to supplant their natural, human insecurities with an inner acceptance and outer expression of true, universal love. That ability enables them to more freely express creativity and increase their capacity to integrate with the energy of our higher purposes as a universal human family.

"As we move to an awareness of our Oneness," George stated, "we can finally begin to contribute to one another's benefits on a global scale, and it all stems from entering that space of genuine self-love."

Healing Insights from Massage, the Chakras, and Beyond

We spoke with holistic healing practitioner Leslie Ray, who gleans much of her intuitive healing guidance from the ability to perceive energy lines, called meridians, in the body. She explained the process: "I literally 'see' the lines when I choose to. And I know when the energy flow is blocked or unhealthy, because it dims down. I can actually see a darkening spot in one area or another. The color of a healthy meridian/energy line is usually a bluish shade."

We asked Leslie to describe what she does when she wants to "see" someone's meridian energy flow. She explained that it is a simple matter of breath and intent. She moves with her breathing into a relaxed state, focusing on the area of concern, all the while holding the mental intention of being of help to the client. That intent, she emphasized, is extremely crucial. The desire to be of service is what Leslie feels allows her to intercede for the person and to gather information about the condition of the client's body, mind, and spirit.

"You can always get results when you place your attention on a chakra . . . To get to the first layer of [a client's] auric field, you can actually focus on your first chakra field and just get there in a snap."

We asked Leslie if she meant that she focused on her *own* chakra field and she answered: "Yes, I focus on what it feels like in that first chakra, and I finally realized after many years of practice that I had been automatically doing that for a long time. Through this method, I can palpably feel any messages that might come up for you [the client] in that area. [If there are blockages] I may receive specific things to tell you from your guides, from your Higher Self, or from my own guides. It's not a command, although once in a while I've heard statements clearly; usually it's just a knowingness . . . I don't say anything to the client until I hear the message over and over again, and if their guides or my guides want to get a message across, they'll make sure I convey it properly."

Because Leslie's approach to healing is very eclectic (she is trained in full-body massage, shiatsu, Shinti, and several other modalities), we wondered how she knows what method to use with each person. She said that she speaks with the client for a while before the treatment in order to attune with the client's energy. She senses, though she cannot explain how, the right thing to do. Once the treatment begins, the insights she receives go beyond the physical problem that the client has.

"Physical problems are always so secondary—they have little to do with the core reason. The core reason is why they come to see me in the first place . . . Especially if I'm doing a physical massage . . . touching every muscle, I'm much more in tune with the physical body at that point. Sometimes I have literally felt something going on in an ankle, an ovary, or a Fallopian tube. I've felt it physically when I was doing energy work, but most of the time . . . I put that aside. There are reasons why the physical condition occurred, and I try to deal with the reason, the root cause of the blockage or ailment."

Leslie's statement sums up clearly what the Cayce readings say about healing, that we can never fully heal a condition until we address the initial cause of it, whether physical, emotional, or mental in nature. She continued:

"There is a natural energy flow that takes place within each person. We are constantly sending energy out and then taking it in. But, sometimes, I can feel energy going out, but it's not being allowed to come back in, or vice versa . . . Many times I will just allow that to continue because it is part of a process the person is going through more than anything else. If a condition is severe, I will consciously send energy to a blocked area to get the flow started again."

Leslie first discovered her abilities to pick up intuitive feelings and to heal people when she was just a small child.

"I had a grandmother who really loved me—I was her favorite—and she sometimes got a little upset with other things in life, as we all do. One time I remember in particular is when I was about five years old . . . I have always been able to 'see' energy, and I recall feeling that if

I sat very close to my grandmother and thought of how much I loved her, her mood would change; it would literally change her. And I distinctly remember being aware of that movement of feeling."

She experienced her ability to give hands-on healing when she was eighteen years old.

"My mother was very ill and became wheelchairbound. I started using my hands at that point for massaging her so that she wouldn't become atrophied; she was ill for eleven years. That was the first real caring that I expressed consistently every day using my hands to help heal."

We asked Leslie to share anything that she has found particularly helpful spiritually in applying her intuitive insights on a professional and personal level. Her response was inspiring:

"I have found that there are different things that I have believed in and moved through during my life, and as long as I kept my heart pure and did things because I felt they were the right thing to do—and remained willing to let anything that didn't reflect that purity out of my life—then I could only become stronger and stronger in everything that I do."

Laying On of Hands:
Prayer and Meditation as Tools of Healing

In her book, *Healing Through Meditation and Prayer*, Meredith Ann Puryear, who practices a method of healing from the readings called "laying on of hands," includes a very important quote from the Cayce material. It deals with the interconnectedness of our different levels of being, as well as the role our attitudes play in affecting our own health and healing—two primary reasons why people seek psychic readings. Those individuals seeking spiritual insight and healing through the realms of prayer and laying on of hands need to be particularly cognizant of this interrelatedness of the various aspects of ourselves and of how integral a part our intent and attitudes play in the whole process.

In thy body—ye find body, mind, soul; or the spiritual, mental and material body. The misapplication of truth in thy mind, in not interpreting the spirit in self, may—as in thine own experience—bring the lack of proper elimination of drosses from thy body.

It is true that ye may in the spiritual, in the mental, in the material, make applications of that cleansing that may aid the body in eliminating same from the physical, from the mental, from the spiritual. The spirit is ever willing, and it remains the same yesterday, today and forever. For it is the eternal spiritual law.

First, then, the mental attitude towards self, towards the world, towards others, must be changed. For, if ye recognize in self the truth, that which is and was manifested in the Christ Consciousness, ye will change thy mental attitude—towards self, towards others, towards conditions about thee. *Then* ye may see change in the physical results or manifestations in self. 3078-1

Meredith's comments on these words are quite succinct: "We see in this reading the hard question that was always directed to a person seeking physical healing: Why do you want to be healed? What are you going to do with health once you achieve it? Are you going to use your body for selfishness, self-centeredness, or do you have some purpose of service?" She then quotes a very profound statement from the readings which says: " . . . there is little need for attempting to heal an ill body unless the mind, the purpose, the ideal of the entity is set in Him who is peace, life, hope and understanding." (3078-1)

Meredith's initial interest in the Cayce material was focused on meditation and prayer, and while living in Texas, she became involved with a prayer healing group at her Presbyterian church. Several members of the group decided to use the laying-on-of-hands method of healing with a number of epileptic children in the area. Although they didn't see dramatic results from their efforts, Meredith felt they made enough progress to keep her interested in the tremendous potential of that healing modality.

She and her family moved to Virginia Beach, where Meredith joined the Glad Helpers Prayer Group, which met and continues to meet at A.R.E. headquarters. By the spring of 1969, they had incorporated the laying on of hands into the weekly healing sessions.

"I'm really convinced that anything can be healed. Cayce says it may take seven years, but it can be healed, so time and patience are often required . . . On occasion, the readings say it may take two seven-year cycles to completely heal certain afflictions."

In commenting on her own ability to heal, Meredith explains: "I don't think I came in as a born healer. I think the tendency was there and certainly the interest. But I really feel it is something I developed. Something that, because I was interested in and committed to [it], I knew [it] would enable me to help people. And I believe the key is . . . working with the ideal, with meditation, prayer . . . your dream life, and with application. I think that anyone who is willing to take the time to be silent and be with God begins this process of attunement or at-one-ment. And, as you do that . . . the Creative Forces begin to flow . . . Whatever area you are working in will be enhanced."

Insight and Service Through Intuitive Psychometry

Mary Roach began giving intuitive readings in the early 1980s. She uses a technique called psychometry, which she described as "holding onto jewelry, car keys, or photographs, for example, and getting ideas or impressions from the object."

She realized as a child that she was extremely sensitive and had an interest in metaphysical subjects. In the early '80s, she took some developmental training classes. "It involved a lot of self-exploration," Mary explained, "figuring out who I was and feeling somewhat clearer about that . . . As we did more and more exercises in intuitive/psychic growth, we eventually moved into the realm of healing, and I realized that what helped me a great deal was positive feedback. Initially, everyone thinks he or she can't really get valid information. But as I continued to be told that my insights were accurate, it encouraged me to continue."

Mary added that her orientation also involved meditation and prayer, as well as confronting issues of forgiveness.

"One exercise involved writing down everybody in your life against whom you still held a grudge and then working to release it. That deeper, emotional, soul-level examination of my inner self gave me the foundation I needed."

The Cayce readings touch on this idea many times. The following excerpts stress how important it is not to become overly enamored by the phenomenality of psychic development but, rather, to focus on the heart of the matter.

> The entity is very unusual; very intuitive; very psychic. The entity should be associated or affiliated closely with those who study such from the

spiritual angle, and not as phenomena only. 2346-1

Thus the intuitions are well, provided those are tempered in spirituality—not ism. 2539-2

We asked Mary to relate what she believes are the most important elements of giving helpful, accurate intuitive guidance. "I've got three things that I think . . . make it easier to tap into psychic information. One is sensitivity. I had an overabundance of sensitivity as I was growing up . . . but it's a great thing to have once it's focused properly. A second quality is empathy. You've got to be more interested in the other person during that time frame than you are in yourself. You've got to be able to be genuinely committed to helping him or her, wanting to do something to make that person's life better. And the third element is . . . that it's good to have some idea of God or Spirit— recognizing that the insights are coming from that higher realm and not just from me. If people are naturally attracted to creative, spiritual endeavors, those elements frequently manifest as the more feminine side of things, such as being receptive and nurturing to others."

In some respects, Mary feels that her intuitive/psychic abilities developed because of "natural flaws" with which she was born. She explains: "I got into this field partly because I didn't have a very strong identity, and it has taken me a long time to feel my own sense of that . . . But to be a good intuitive, you have to get out of your own way. You have to be able to disappear. This was initially very easy for me because I didn't have a strong ego/ identity to work from, so I could disappear automatically. Now I've developed more of my own identity, but I can still get out of the way. Otherwise, there is always the danger of indulging in the power of it and not putting your own ego aside."

Intuitive information comes to Mary in various ways, but she is particularly interested in helping people find their life's purpose or mission. "I usually start with where the person is, where one's life direction is . . . I can't always control how it starts. Sometimes an angel will come in first . . . Other times I will see an important past-life experience for that person. But usually it's the life direction first; it's like a map. You are here. Then this is what's summed up, and finally these are the possible trends for you.

"I think I'm more programmed toward the soul's direction and why we're here—emotional issues, past lives—I love that sort of thing. So, when people ask me about karma or relationship questions, it is really fun for me, and it just flows. I also find it rewarding to see some healing as a result of the insights that come.

"The actual procedure I follow is that I hold the client's jewelry or watch in my left hand . . . it feels very uncomfortable in my right hand. For me, the left is receptive; the right is outgoing. Then, I always say prayers. I begin with some [traditional] prayers and then proceed with a specific, more personalized prayer that uses the individual's name and age, a prayer which is just between me and God. I always say, 'Please,' and I ask to receive information that would help the person and that the person's soul would tell me what would be good for him or her to know at this time. Once I feel centered, I always ask Jesus to come in, and He is very obliging in that way . . . His presence allows me to act as a conduit of communication. Then I will invite in angels or guides to help me interpret the messages I am getting."

There is also a period of waiting. "Once I've done prayers and the requests for this particular person," Mary explained, "I wait until images, words, or concepts start to come through. It's not like I'm just thinking . . . It's too fast for my thought processes—almost like unraveling a huge ball of yarn."

Ultimately, if the person requesting the reading is sincere in wanting to improve a life situation and is open to the information that comes through, whether it's via an angel, deceased loved one, or one's own higher self, Mary feels confident that the necessary guidance will be given.

A Journey to the Hall of Records: Steps Along the Path to Insight

When Edgar Cayce gave life readings for individuals, he frequently got his information from what was alternately called the akashic records, God's Book of Remembrance, and the hall of records. The following excerpt is a verbatim account given by Cayce at a public lecture of what he experienced in an altered state:

I see myself as a tiny dot out of my physical body, which lies inert before me. I find myself oppressed by darkness and there is a feeling of terrific loneliness. Suddenly, I am conscious of a white beam of light. As this tiny dot, I move upward following the light, knowing that I must follow it or be lost.

As I move along this path of light I gradually become conscious of various levels upon which there is movement. Upon the first levels there are vague, horrible shapes, grotesque forms such as one sees in nightmares. Passing on, there begin to appear on either side misshapen forms of human beings with some part of the body magnified. Again there is change and I become conscious of gray-hooded forms moving downward. Gradually, these become lighter in color. Then the direction changes and these forms move upward and the color of the robes grows rapidly lighter. Next, there begin to appear on either side vague outlines of houses, walls, trees, etc., but everything is motionless. As I pass on, there is more light and movement in what appear to be normal cities and towns. With the growth of movement I become conscious of sounds, at first indistinct rumblings, then music, laughter, and singing of birds. There is more and more light, the colors become very beautiful, and there is the sound of wonderful music. The houses are left behind, ahead there is only a blending of sound and color. Quite suddenly I come upon a hall of records. It is a hall without walls, without ceiling, but I am conscious of seeing an old man who hands me a large book, a record of the individual for whom I seek information. 294-19 Reports

Variations of this process were described in other writings of Mr. Cayce as well as in several of his readings. It seems significant to note that the gathering of psychic information is not an altogether pleasant experience, as Cayce's description of the initial levels will attest, and this explains why Cayce began each session with a period of prayer. However, it seems to be a symbolic path that he followed, which required him to encounter negative images—quite real on the astral plane—before he could move on to the place where beautiful colors, music, and enlightened beings appear. The intuitive process was multifaceted for Cayce. It is lucky for us that he chose to brave those sometimes terrifying experiences in order to reach the space where wisdom and knowledge were accessible for those in need.

7

CREATIVITY AND
ITS RELATIONSHIP TO INTUITION

That the soul of each should be a companion with, of, the
Creative Forces, is the purpose of each entity, each soul.

261-15

TO LOOK UPON OURSELVES as companions of the Creator, as the quote above suggests, is to recognize that, as souls, we are in essence *creative* beings. As we attune to that purpose, we become cognizant of our souls' expression manifesting through intuitive vibrations and awareness. There is an interconnectedness between our creativity and the intuitive impulses that operate through us as physical conduits of spiritual light or energy.

We do not always realize the full impact behind the term *creativity,* nor do we seem to comprehend the fact that to be creative we must sometimes be truly courageous. We are each expressing an aspect of ourselves every time we make a choice in life, no matter how big or small it might be; making a choice is, in the truest sense of the word, being creative. Decisions can require courage at times, because they are frequently unprecedented in our personal experience. This seems particularly true when we first begin to use our intuitive faculties, because the outcome is unknown. Acting creatively in those unexplored, untested moments of human endeavor is comparable to jumping into a great void and hoping for the best.

For that reason, it is much less intimidating to think of creativity in a detached way, tending to view it as something that occurs only on special occasions or to certain artistically inclined individuals. Artists are wonderful role models for the expression of creative energy, and we draw upon their insights throughout this chapter; however, it is a limiting perspective to think that only artists are creative.

As we respond to various influences and promptings throughout the day (and night), we are allowing the expression of our true creative nature as spiritual beings. Some responses are easier to make than others, and under certain circumstances, our responses (choices) can be downright painful.

Creativity Isn't Just for Artists

Perhaps it is the beauty of artistic expression that causes us to consider only the arts as being *creative.* Therefore, unless we are artists ourselves, we may believe creativity to be something separate and outside of ourselves, and associate it with unattainable perfection and beauty without seeing the connection between it and our own intuitive spirit.

In reality, creativity can just as easily be born during

mundane daily activities. Its impact is determined by the quality of our individual intent or mindfulness during those activities and not so much by what we consider to be significant or insignificant. Creativity is so much a part of us, being initiated by the use of our free wills, that we can't always see the forest for the trees.

This idea of being creative in everyday circumstances was reinforced in an interview with accomplished artist and teacher, Meryl Ann Butler. She commented on the large number of her art students over the years who were "convinced they don't have an artistic or creative bone in their bodies." When students express that belief, she asks them, "Have you ever raised a family?" Most of them answer in the affirmative. Meryl Ann's response to them is, "Well, you know what? That's the one thing in my life that has taken more creativity than anything else. More than my artwork or anything." For Meryl Ann, "Raising a family of seven . . . forced me into finding *a lot* of creative solutions . . . "

Cliff Selover, another successful artist who currently works in advertising, illustrates this capacity to use creativity as a problem-solving tool. He explained, "Problem solving is an intuitive, emotional process in a cognitive, rational framework . . . Our work is to create solutions that have to communicate to people. So we need to know how to communicate on the emotional and intuitive levels. What is most meaningful to them and how do we convey that? It involves [all the levels] . . . with intuitive perception . . . giving focus and meaning to the creative response."

Dr. Henry Reed commented on the interrelationship between creativity and intuition. One major point he touched upon is the impact of an individual's intention and motivation in gathering meaningful information intuitively and then expressing the insights creatively. He views the process as "getting out of your own way" (as was discussed in the previous chapter), and having the "freedom to be spontaneous with a purpose." For example, when a painter creates a work of art, the end result is not usually produced in a matter of moments (although it might appear to be done spontaneously) but is a culminating process over a period of time, through a series of choices, focused upon a desired outcome—whether that outcome is consciously recognized or not. It is unlikely that each brush stroke is made from a purely conscious state of mind. Many of those choices probably come from an unconscious level and are guided by their creator's intent and focused ideal. An internal knowing germinates within the artist of what is desired—the result of that "knowing" shows up on the canvas. This is the point where *inspiration* comes into effect.

As Reed perceives it, "Most creative people learn that they have to use what they have at hand. Whereas the average person may wait for the muse to strike, the professionally creative person or psychic can't afford to wait for the muse to appear; these people might rely on some methods that they can just draw upon that they have come to trust . . . like the improvisational actor to whom you give a sentence or scene, and he or she just begins to perform."

What he is referring to here, in part, is the idea of imagination—letting fleeting thoughts, images, or ideas take hold and carry you through to the full impact of the psychic messages you might be receiving. He stresses the importance of being "aware and mindful . . . opening oneself to the moment and allowing one's own interpretation of immediate circumstances to help [one] gain insight." Following in this same vein, the Cayce readings suggest that anyone who is very imaginative is also very psychic.

In the previous chapter we heard from professional intuitive Mary Roach, who believes one of the key factors in her ability to receive intuitive guidance is the fact that she is highly imaginative. So a good imagination combined with the other characteristics she mentioned—sensitivity, empathy, and recognition of a higher power—add to the level of creativity. Cliff Selover reiterated this idea. Before he begins any artistic endeavor, he first imagines "a lot of possibilities . . . I see it in my mind's eye. [I] run through the various possibilities before deciding 'this is it' . . . Being open to imagination allows the possibility of intuitive thought to enter and then lead you somewhere new. As you create it, it takes on a life of its own . . . Sometimes things are better when they turn out differently than you first imagined."

Inspiration in the Harmony of Life

Because the arts and music demonstrate so clearly the marriage of intuition and creativity, we asked professional musician and songwriter Anna Lee Scully to describe how her creative process is expressed in relation to her intuitive abilities. Invariably, Anna Lee said, ideas for lyrics or melodies for songs come to her as the result of experience. Whether the experience is as simple as meeting a new person, seeing a beautiful scene in nature, or being drawn to a particular article in the newspaper, something moving in that experience leads Anna Lee to express it creatively. At times, those resonant experiences come back randomly into her consciousness long after the actual experience first takes place.

"I feel there needs to be what I would call a void or space of emptiness in my life in order to truly be creative," Anna Lee said. "If the mundane aspects of the day take all my energy, I find it very difficult to funnel the inspirational responses into a focused space of expression. Simplifying my life, setting boundaries, and finding balance for myself and an opportunity to be in silence for a time are essential to me. While I am performing, I'm in that totally responsive, intuitive space that allows me to attune to that [surge of expression] that's been dormant within me."

Once she experiences what she calls "that shift in perspective," it just seems to flow of its own volition. However, it's crucial in the creative process, she emphasizes, to "always know when it's time to quit." This is an intuitive aspect of creativity, because no one can tell you when to stop: You just have to know it on a gut level. This is something that many people notice through the medium of film. Probably everyone has had the experience of enjoying a movie until it starts to bog down and becomes sluggish or boring. Once the creative statement has been expressed, its energy can only be prolonged for a certain period of time without becoming redundant. This is when the artist/intuitive must apply both discernment and personal interpretation of *truth* to the piece of art, music, or psychic reading being rendered at that moment.

Can Seclusion Lead to Creative Freedom?

Kreg Scully, Anna Lee's husband, is an accomplished artist, sculptor, and gemologist who described his intuitive/creative process as "training" himself to wake up. Simply *beginning* to create, not knowing where it might lead, is a key factor, Kreg said. Sometimes putting himself through intense circumstances can trigger a change in his state of awareness, leading to the freedom needed to fully express his art.

One method is closing himself into a room for lengthy periods of time, with no visual stimuli (no basket of fruit for a still life, no beautiful scenery viewed from a window), until he produces something tangible. In this way, he is forced to rely on inner inspiration for the subject of his creations, which frequently come from the contents of his dreams or intuitive memories. He discovered, too, that the simple act of picking up his paintbrush and starting to paint often stimulates dream recall. This is similar to Cliff Selover's process of "just going into the studio, opening the materials . . . smelling the paint and starting to work" that seems to trigger creative movement.

Scully finds that, while in his self-imposed seclusion, a breakthrough often occurs and the "art" then begins to flow in earnest. Up until that point, he previously would question what he was putting on the canvas; but he trained himself to stop censoring and to just allow it to happen. Getting to the point where he could "awaken patience" within himself is how Kreg described his connection to the Higher Creative Forces.

This idea is mirrored in a biblical phrase and a Cayce study group reading that states: "In patience possess ye your soul." (262-26) We must be willing to wait for Spirit to move us at times, and it doesn't always move us when we would like. That is why Kreg, Meryl Ann, and other professionals with whom we spoke feel it is so important to meditate and pray often in order to truly attune to the Creative Spirit.

Kreg also suggested trying to view the world from the perspective of a small child, without all the trappings of our "adult" reality. He recalled an intuitive experience at the age of seven, when he felt totally in tune with nature. As he was walking in the woods, enjoying his surroundings, he felt a tremendous urge to stop where he was and start digging in the dirt. Being an innocent child, Kreg never questioned that impulse. He simply started digging and eventually found an old coin dating back to the Civil War period. That childlike sense of unquestionable *knowing* is what Kreg tries to emulate as he creates his works of art.

Indeed, that quality of innocent wonder might be

what Jesus was talking about when He said, "Until you become as one of these little ones, you cannot enter the kingdom of heaven."

Wisdom Culled from the Words of Well-Known Artists

Another perspective on inspiration alluding to our individual or personal connection to the Creative Force comes from well-known British author D.H. Lawrence. In an article entitled "Making Pictures," he commented on his attempts at becoming a painter after decades of working as a writer. Whatever mode of expression an artist employs, he said, it all comes from the same source anyway.

"It needs a certain purity of spirit to be an artist, of any sort . . . An artist may be a profligate . . . from the social point of view . . . But if he can paint a nude woman, or a couple of apples, so that they are a living image, then he was pure in spirit, and, for the time being, his was the kingdom of heaven. This is the beginning of all art, visual, literary or musical: be pure in spirit. It isn't the same as goodness. It is much more difficult and nearer the divine. The divine isn't only good, it is all things." (Taken from *The Creative Process*, edited by Brewster Ghiselin for Mentor books.)

This same process affects us every moment of every day as we go about our normal routines, no matter the nature of our endeavors. But how we set the stage, through the use of ideals and the application of spiritual practices, in large part determines the quality of our creations. Growth occurs as we become more expansive in our thinking and realize that creativity permeates every aspect of our existence. We are creating our lives as we go along, through the use of our intuitive faculties.

Paramahansa Yogananda, world-famous author of *Autobiography of a Yogi* and founder of the Self-Realization Fellowship, describes creativity in a very beautiful way, reinforcing the necessity of taking initiative in order to get the creative process flowing. "The unlimited Creative Principle within you is the source of all art and wisdom. When you want to create something important, sit quietly and meditate deeply upon it. You will be guided by the creative Spirit, but you should also exercise determination in accomplishing your objective. Awaken initiative, which is the creative faculty within you—a spark from the divine Creator. You must do something which will show that God's creative principle is active within you."

It's essential, also, not to be misled into thinking that creativity always evolves under the best or most pleasant of circumstances, but to recognize that great beauty can be born of tremendous pain or suffering. Many famous artists are known for the difficult, sometimes tortured lives they have led. Yet, their creations live on after centuries, still serving as beacons of inspiration and representing the wonder of human potential.

Vincent Van Gogh experienced such profound mental and physical anguish that he literally cut off his own ear. Yet, his works of art are considered some of the finest in the world.

Mozart and his family were impoverished during his later years, and still he managed to create what many consider the most magnificent music of all time. Perhaps this came about as a result of his response to the frustrating and humbling circumstances in his physical world.

Mozart's intuitive creations apparently came to him as flashes of insight rather than as gradual "knowings," as might be experienced by some psychics or artists. This diversity highlights again the beauty of our uniqueness as individual souls.

When Charlotte Brontë, author of the classic work *Jane Eyre,* was growing up in nineteenth-century England, the stiflingly conservative attitudes toward women as writers or artists prevented most women from even attempting to publish their works. But, in spite of tremendous obstacles, she and her sisters, Emily and Anne, found a way to have their works published. They submitted their work with male pseudonyms to the publisher in order to have their material read; and, thankfully, their approach worked. By the time the conservative literary community discovered who the real authors were, it was too late to recant their words of praise for the sisters' novels.

Consider, too, the impact that the reclusive northern England lifestyle led by the Brontë family had on their insights and creative imaginations. Emily, who authored *Wuthering Heights*, reportedly had frequent out-of-body experiences, which most certainly influenced her to write with such etheric, mystical overtones in her haunting novel.

Fortunately, the Brontë sisters and countless others persevered with their creative talents, giving humanity the beautiful insights found within them.

These are examples of how inspiration and creative energy can overcome negative obstacles when the intent to share one's art, one's soul, is strong and pure in its direction. We all have the opportunity to turn our circumstances into what the Cayce readings referred to as "stumbling blocks or stepping stones." Frequently, we receive creative promptings through guidance transmitted by way of our intuitive perceptions.

Carl G. Jung, renowned psychologist and contemporary of both Edgar Cayce and Sigmund Freud, explained the interrelationship between the artist and the viewer of the art in his groundbreaking book, *Modern Man in Search of a Soul.*

" . . . the work of the [artist] comes to meet the spiritual need of the society in which he lives . . . Being essentially the instrument for his work, he is subordinate to it, and we have no reason for expecting him to interpret it for us. He has done the best that in him lies in giving it form, and he must leave the interpretation to others and to the future. A great work of art is like a dream; for all its apparent obviousness it does not explain itself and is never unequivocal."

Must We Struggle?

We asked Henry Reed to comment on our observation that true art and intuitive insights frequently seem to stem from states of depression or traumatic experiences, and we asked if he saw an interrelatedness between them. His in-depth response brings to the surface an important element in the realm of intuitive development, the setting of boundaries:

"There is actually a triangle of connectivity that you are asking about here. One point is creativity, another is psychic, and the other is . . . symptomology—psychopathology, problems, something of that sort. The genius-in-madness question on one hand, the disturbed psychic on another . . . and the psychic creativity—those are your different combinations in that triangle, and they all are related.

"One of the things that they all have in common has to do with personal boundaries and transpersonal boundaries. When you [move] beyond your own personal boundaries, then you can be creative. New ideas can come up that you haven't been exposed to, you can go beyond yourself. You can be intuitive, that is, you can get insights that seem to come from beyond your own experience. You can get psychic information that goes beyond your personal experience. And you can be haunted or driven by forces that seem to be out of control . . . So the madness, the sense of the person who is possessed by the gods . . . was the way mental illness used to be [viewed]—as an affliction of the gods. And in some cultures, like Native American, societies would . . . honor those people, because they knew that whatever made that person kind of crazy . . . would also make that person creative, psychic, and an asset to the community."

As Reed pointed out, depression is not the only touchstone to dynamic creativity:

"You have to recognize that there are lots of other people who are and were creative when they weren't depressed, and they were much happier than the ones who were creative while being depressed—and perhaps their creative efforts were even more meaningful . . . The link among mysticism, madness, and genius doesn't mean that madness or problems are the only way to accomplish creative acts.

"We should also realize that for many creative/psychic people, joy, celebration, and positive attunement can be devotional paths to creativity and intuition. We don't want to romanticize the bad stuff . . . although there's no doubt that mental illness can bring into being the wounded healer, who proceeds to heal wounds and then lead you to a creative, intuitive space. But, on the more desirable side of that can be the ecstatic healer/intuitive who heals from a joyful, uplifted mode."

Both Selover and Butler support the idea of not being traumatized in order to create. Cliff says he often wakes up with dream images or impressions that seem to come in response to the project he's working on, and there are physical indicators that tell him he's on the right track—a tingling sensation or sense of excitement, as if something wonderful is about to happen. Meryl Ann relates her creativity to the level of "passion and love" that she feels for the subject. She uses Jesus as an example of someone who was "passionate about His life's purpose. He showed how we can break through [the status quo] paradigm by having passion for whatever we do." That passion engenders creative expression.

There are two optimal ways, Reed said, to enhance spontaneous creativity without having to override our inhibitions with drugs or alcohol. Those methods are *play* and *pretend.* They allow individuals to be loose and flexible, without feeling threatened or out of control.

Playing and pretending are excellent ways to relax the mind without being distracted by worries or concerns. This is one reason we believe there is so much value in doing creative activities, such as hobbies. You focus your attention on the activity, whether it be acting in a play, gardening, repairing cars, knitting a sweater, or dancing—whatever brings joy to your heart. When you perform that activity, you are opening the channel of intuitive energy that is ever present within. You are choosing to channel it in a positive direction and, as you do so, your body, mind, and spirit all operate in balance with one another. This is what's known as living in the moment—what Eastern philosophers might call a Zen state. Being "at one" permits the Creative Forces to act through you as a conduit of cocreatorship.

We can take advantage of that all-present source of energy for ourselves by being aware of bits of wisdom that surface in daily circumstances and by taking responsibility for the lifestyle or path we choose to embrace. As we make the effort to attune ourselves to the Higher Forces through meditation, prayer, and the application of a loving attitude toward others, we can feel confident that we are opening avenues of intuitive insight that lead to our creative essence. Intuition works hand in hand with creative expression, one enhancing the other.

A Day in the Life of a Spiritual Seeker

If we examine the activities that generally take place on any given day, we can see how varied our circumstances and responses to them might be. To clarify the way it all works together, let's go through a hypothetical day right now. This should illustrate the types of choices with which we are typically presented and how we might choose to apply our insights and creativity in responding to the situations given.

Please keep in mind that there are no wrong or right answers here. In fact, on certain days, it may actually feel appropriate to make a choice that could be judged as "unenlightened" on another occasion. Whatever the case may be, try to be honest with yourself as you go through these hypothetical situations, and then see how your overall response feels as a result.

• You wake up to your alarm, sensing the vestiges of a dream in your memory. Some sample response options are: (1) Lie there for a few moments retrieving the feelings and details of the dream and then write down what you remember; (2) review the dream thoroughly in your mind before getting out of bed and then continue to examine it as you go about your morning routine; (3) go back to sleep and try to continue the dream; (4) panic about being on time for work and jump out of the bed, allowing the dream to flit out of your consciousness entirely.

• Your carpool ride calls to say she'll be fifteen minutes late, so you use the extra time in one of the following ways: (1) Turn on the TV to see the morning news and feel somewhat depressed as a result; (2) go to your special space and meditate for ten minutes; (3) eat another doughnut, even though you're trying to improve your diet; (4) complain about the driver being late again until you become really angry.

• A co-worker passes you in the hallway, and you

sense that he is feeling rather down. Your response options are: (1) Decide to leave him alone to work it out and continue walking; (2) exchange pleasantries in a nonthreatening way, allowing your co-worker to share his burden if he chooses; (3) say a quick prayer and walk away; (4) tell the person you've picked up a depressed feeling from him and ask what the matter is.

• A business client phones and angrily explains that she's upset by the delay in receiving her order from your company. You know the delay isn't your fault, but in explaining the situation accurately, you would need to reveal the incompetence of a co-worker. You are tired of taking the blame for another person's mistakes, but you don't want to discredit your organization. Your response options are: (1) Apologize and promise to get the items mailed immediately, while deciding to let things slide with your co-worker, who seems to be impossible to change; (2) apologize, explaining that it's not your fault, then transfer her call to the person who made the mistake, catching him unprepared; (3) explain that there were unforeseen circumstances in the department and that you will expedite the order; then talk with the co-worker, explaining that you will not cover for him again; (4) tell the client who it was that caused the delay and then complain to the co-worker's superior; (5) say a quick silent prayer to calm yourself and the client; then promise to follow through with the order, allowing the universe to take care of the co-worker's behavior.

• It's nearing the end of the work day, and you're looking forward to exercising at the gym. You get a phone call from a friend who tends to always have a "bad day" and wants to meet you at a bar after work to talk about it. Your response options are: (1) Tell her you are sick of hearing about all her problems and that she needs to stop being so negative; (2) say that you really need to work out first, but you'll call her later and talk on the phone; (3) go to the bar with her even though you really don't want to and don't particularly enjoy bars; (4) tell her you'll meet her there in order to avoid turning her down, then leave a message on her machine later saying you couldn't make it at the last minute; (5) invite your friend to work out with you to get rid of her negative feelings of the day and then suggest having dinner afterwards to talk; (6) get to the gym, decide in the parking lot that you're being a bad friend, and then go to the bar and feel miserable all night because you haven't exercised.

In assessing your responses to the above scenarios, did you feel happy with the choices you made, or did you sense that a "less than perfect" day ensued (from a spiritual perspective) as a result? Perhaps you created different responses than ours that seemed more likely in your daily activities. If so, did you feel that those responses were taking you in a more constructive direction with your behavior than you have been headed in the past?

Whatever your overall sense about this hypothetical day, use that understanding to evaluate your own intuitive/creative level of awareness. Did you see how certain choices might seem OK temporarily, but in the long run would be more confusing or detrimental in the effect they might have? For example, if you made the choice to leave a message for the friend who wanted you to go to the bar, instead of telling her directly how you felt, do you see how that would only prolong the issue and not do either of you any good ultimately? Being dishonest even on a seemingly simple level can have a potentially unhealthy effect on your soul growth as well as your friend's.

Intuitive Creativity in Action

Acting on our intuitive or psychic impressions takes on greater import if we view it as the method in which we express our souls. It might be helpful to examine the way two individuals responded to intuitive perceptions in their lives; in both cases, the events seemed insignificant when they occurred but, in retrospect, were highly meaningful.

A young man named Michael had been considering a career change even though he was doing well in his chosen profession. He had been praying to find the best direction in which to head, since his interests and talents were quite diverse. One day a new client, Louis, came into his office. Michael was struck by his kind demeanor and upbeat attitude. Louis mentioned offhandedly that he didn't want to be late for his evening yoga class at a local recreation center. Michael had felt a sudden warmth in his hands and in the area of his heart upon meeting Louis and sensed that he would benefit from getting to know Louis better. Michael decided to attend that night's yoga session. As a result of that choice, the two became good friends, and Michael learned yoga so well that he eventually became an instructor and opened his own school. The career change he had been looking for happened in a totally unexpected manner because he was willing to take a *creative* step in response to his intuitive prompting.

Yvette was a young mother with two small children. She and her husband had just moved to a new rural community, and without her own car she was feeling a bit isolated and disconnected from adult companionship. As she was reading to her five-year-old daughter one morning, a fortuitous insight occurred. Her daughter mentioned how the character in the book looked a lot like the older lady who lived a few houses down the road from them. The instant she heard those words, Yvette felt a rush of energy go up her spine and a numbness in the top of her head. In the future, she came to realize the importance of that feeling. Based on her daughter's remark, Yvette paid a visit to the lady down the road that afternoon with wonderful results. It turned out that the woman had recently had surgery and was unable to drive her car in order to run errands and so forth. She was pleased to discover that Yvette was quite willing to drive her to the store, and Yvette was more than happy for the company and the opportunity to be of service at the same time.

These examples may seem simplistic at first glance, but the final outcome in both scenarios did a great deal to improve the circumstances of everyone involved. Just by responding to intuitive guidance, both Michael and Yvette became creative participants in their own lives. That is what cocreativity is all about.

Awakening to the Real You:
Creating and Enjoying Your Life's Path

We have covered ideas in this book that we hope will impact your personal future in intuitive development, whatever form it takes. But the final and probably most important step on the path to soul growth is the decision to take action—what the Cayce readings touch upon again and again: *application!*

Offering the following steps as a closing guideline, we wish you well in undertaking the adventure of your own soul's journey. Glance at these suggestions from each chapter of the book and choose at least one *new* practice to incorporate into your regular routine:

- Meditate each day for at least five minutes.
- Set and write down your spiritual ideal.
- Become more conscientious about a healthful diet.
- Visit a Search for God study group.
- Choose one or two modes of intuitive expression with which you resonate and then consciously seek to enhance it. For example, if you feel that you are tele-

pathic, experiment with a friend by having that friend send you messages, and vice versa.

• Incubate a dream for guidance.

• Make a list of the cultures to which you are attracted. Choose one with which you feel a positive connection and bring elements of that culture into your daily activities.

• Review your own intuitive experiences and evaluate your impressions, how you received them, and in what way they influenced you or were helpful. Notice how you became aware that the information was intuitive. What physical indicators, if any, did you experience? Did some action or practice on your part or a traumatic event initiate the experience?

• Find a way to use your intuitive capacities positively in your own occupation.

• Try a new hobby or activity that intrigues you.

Conclusion

Based upon the insights conveyed in this chapter, creativity might be described as putting our intuition into action, applying what we know to do, and appreciating our own essence as a unique part of the Creative Whole. As the following Cayce reading excerpt suggests, being who we truly are as souls on the earth is the best that any individual can hope to accomplish in a lifetime.

Keep, then, the faith in those Creative Forces that make for the *beauty* of Life. As the life is *lived,* so does it become as a guide; not as that said, but that *done!* For what ye are speaks louder than what ye say! 990-1

Enjoy creating your own process of awakening!

Afterword

The history of humanity is filled with reasons to be inspired, joyful, and proud of our heritage on the earth. But there are also historical events that cause justifiable concern about our future as a race on this planet. How we choose to view that legacy of human endeavor is up to us. And our perceptions of the past will have a distinct impact on the way our future evolves.

The "real you" is a unique and intuitive being with a tremendous capacity to create positive change in the world. We can decide to emphasize our own strengths for the betterment of our planet and its inhabitants—or we can choose to contribute to its potential detriment if we allow fear or lack of trust to rule our actions.

What will we decide? It is hoped that the ideas presented here will encourage us to appreciate one another as parts of the greater Whole and to express our individual talents and abilities fully, even when it is difficult to do so. But will our efforts to grow personally lead us a crucial step further? Will we choose to be supportive of others who are trying to give the best of themselves and refuse to let them get by with anything less?

What shall we leave behind for future generations? If we wield the power of our intuitive insights with love, compassion, and understanding, we can bequeath a legacy of beauty, hope, and joyful inspiration, awakening our heritage as the freedom-loving spirits we were created to be.

Our future really is up to us, as we hope this book illustrates. So let us accept our responsibility with willing hearts and purposefully awakened spirits.

APPENDIX I

Affirmations from the Study Group Readings

THESE AFFIRMATIONS ARE TAKEN verbatim from the Edgar Cayce readings. In his personal life, Cayce was a dedicated student of the Bible and a devout Christian. Oftentimes, the wording of the readings reflected his own background and the culture in which he lived in the early twentieth century. Feel free to modify or personalize these affirmations to make them come alive for you.

Cooperation

Not my will but Thine, O Lord, be done in me and through me. Let me ever be a channel of blessings, today, now, to those that I contact, in every way. Let my going in, mine coming out be in accord with that Thou would have me do. And as the call comes, "Here am I, send me, use me!" (262-3)

Know Thyself

Father, as we seek to see and know Thy face, may we each, as individuals, and as a group, come to know ourselves, even as we are known, that we—as lights in Thee—may give the better concept of Thy Spirit in this world. (262-5)

What Is My Ideal?

God, be merciful to me! Help Thou my unbelief! Let me see in Him that Thou would have me see in my fellow man. Let me see in my brother that I see in Him whom I worship. (262-11)

Faith

Create in me a pure heart, O God. Open Thou mine heart to the faith Thou hast implanted in all that seek Thy face! Help Thou mine unbelief in my God, in my neighbor, in myself! (262-13)

Virtue and Understanding

Let virtue and understanding be in me, for my defense is in Thee, O Lord, my Redeemer; for Thou hearest the prayer of the upright in heart. (262-17)

Fellowship

How excellent is Thy name in the earth, O Lord! Would I have fellowship with Thee, I must show brotherly love to my fellow man. Though I come in humbleness and have aught against my brother, my prayer, my meditation does not rise to Thee. Help Thou my efforts in my approach to thee. (262-21)

Patience
How gracious is Thy presence in the earth, O Lord. Be Thou the guide, that we with patience may run the race which is set before us, looking to Thee, the Author, the Giver of light. (262-24)

The Open Door
As the Father knoweth me, so may I know the Father, through the Christ Spirit, the door to the kingdom of the Father. Show Thou me the way. (262-27)

In His Presence
Our Father, who art in heaven, may Thy kingdom come in earth through Thy presence in me, that the light of Thy word may shine unto those that I meet day by day. May Thy presence in my brother be such that I may glorify Thee. May I so conduct my own life that others may know Thy presence abides with me, and thus glorify Thee. (262-30)

The Cross and the Crown
Our Father, our God, as we approach that that may give us a better insight of what He bore in the cross, what His glory may be in the crown, may Thy blessings—as promised through Him—be with us as we study together in His name. (262-34)

The Lord Thy God Is One
As my body, mind and soul are one, Thou, O Lord, in the manifestations in the earth, in power, in might, in glory, art one. May I see in that I do, day by day, more of that realization, and manifest the more. (262-38)

Love

Our Father, through the love that Thou has manifested in the world through Thy Son, the Christ, make us more aware of "God is love." (262-43)

APPENDIX II

Reading List

Capacchione, Lucia, M.A. *The Power of Your Other Hand*, Hollywood, CA: New Castle Publishing Co, Inc., 1988.

Castaneda, Carlos. *The Art of Dreaming*, New York, NY: Harper Collins, 1993.

Cayce, Edgar. *A Search for God, Book I*, Virginia Beach, VA: A.R.E. Press, 1942.

Ghiselin, Brewster, ed. *The Creative Process*, New York, NY: New American Library, 1952.

Jung, Carl. *Modern Man in Search of a Soul*, New York, NY: Harcourt Brace, and Co., 1933.

Knaster, Mirka. *Discovering the Body's Wisdom*, New York, NY: Bantam Books, 1996.

MacArthur, B., and D. *The Intelligent Heart: Transform Your Life with the Laws of Love*, Virginia Beach, VA: A.R.E. Press, 1997.

MacArthur, Bruce. *Your Life: Why It Is the Way It Is and What You Can Do About It*, Virginia Beach, VA: A.R.E. Press, 1993.

Pagels, Elaine. *The Gnostic Gospels*, New York, NY: Random House, 1979.

Peterson, Richard. *Creative Meditation: Inner Peace Is Practically Yours*, Virginia Beach, VA: A.R.E. Press, 1990.

Puryear, H., and Thurston, M. *Meditation and the Mind of Man*, Virginia Beach, VA: A.R.E. Press, 1975.

Puryear, Meredith. *Healing Through Meditation and Prayer*, Virginia Beach, VA: A.R.E. Press, 1978.

Reed, Henry. *Your Mind: Unlocking Your Hidden Powers*, Virginia Beach, VA: A.R.E. Press, 1996.

Sechrist, Elsie. *Meditation—Gateway to Light*, Virginia Beach, VA: A.R.E. Press, 1964.

Sparrow, Scott. *Lucid Dreaming: Dawning of the Clear Light*, Virginia Beach, VA: A.R.E. Press, 1976.

Thurston, Mark. *Dreams: Tonight's Answers for Tomorrow's Questions*, New York, NY: St. Martin's Press, 1996.

Todeschi, Kevin. *The Edgar Cayce Ideals Workbook: Taking Control of Your Life*, Virginia Beach, VA: A.R.E. Press 1991.

Yogananda. *Autobiography of a Yogi*, New York, NY: Philosophical Library, 1956.

Nancy C. Pohle

Nancy C. Pohle has lectured, counseled, and taught classes on dreams and intuition throughout the U.S. and Canada for more than eighteen years. She was featured internationally on Voice of America radio and appeared on A&E's *Biography: Edgar Cayce* as a representative of the Association for Research and Enlightenment. Nancy served on A.R.E.'s staff in Virginia Beach for seventeen years, including her last position as public information officer. A professional narrator and on-camera spokesperson, Nancy can be heard and seen on numerous audio and video programs. She grew up in a family that discussed dreams daily—a tradition she has shared with her two now-grown daughters and young granddaughter. Nancy is also a fourth-degree black belt in Shotokan karate. She resides in Colorado with her husband, Dennis Chrisbaum, doing freelance writing, lecturing, and voice-over work.

Ellen L. Selover

Ellen L. Selover is a lifelong student of the Edgar Cayce readings. Her tenure on the staff of the Association for Research and Enlightenment, Inc., has included international study group coordinator, manager of youth programs, and program manager with membership and the Mission in Life Institute. Her particular love has been the A.R.E. Camp, where spiritual principles are practiced in practical ways. Ellen is also a graduate of the Cayce/Reilly School of Massotherapy.

Tell us your stories!

Our hope is that the personal experiences in this book will bring to mind instances of your own intuitive insights and dream occurrences. If they do, please share them with us. Write down your experiences and send them to:

Ellen Selover
Association for Research and Enlightenment, Inc.
215 67th Street
Virginia Beach, VA 23451-2061

Include a self-addressed, stamped envelope if you would like to have your material returned. In the event of future publication, please let us know if we have permission to use your story and whether or not you would like us to use your real name. We look forward to hearing from you. Thank you!

A.R.E. PRESS

The A.R.E. Press publishes quality books, videos, and audiotapes meant to improve the quality of our readers' lives—personally, professionally, and spiritually. We hope our products support your endeavors to realize your career potential, to enhance your relationships, to improve your health, and to encourage you to make the changes necessary to live a loving, joyful, and fulfilling life.

For more information or to receive a free catalog, call:

1-800-723-1112

Or write:

A.R.E. Press
215 67th Street
Virginia Beach, VA 23451-2061

DISCOVER HOW THE EDGAR CAYCE MATERIAL CAN HELP YOU!

The Association for Research and Enlightenment, Inc. (A.R.E.®), was founded in 1931 by Edgar Cayce. Its international headquarters are in Virginia Beach, Virginia, where thousands of visitors come year-round. Many more are helped and inspired by A.R.E.'s local activities in their own hometowns or by contact via mail (and now the Internet!) with A.R.E. headquarters.

People from all walks of life, all around the world, have discovered meaningful and life-transforming insights in the A.R.E. programs and materials, which focus on such areas as holistic health, dreams, family life, finding your best vocation, reincarnation, ESP, meditation, personal spirituality, and soul growth in small-group settings. Call us today on our toll-free number:

1-800-333-4499

or

Explore our electronic visitor's center on the
INTERNET: **http://www.are-cayce.com**

We'll be happy to tell you more about how the work of the A.R.E. can help you!

A.R.E.
215 67th Street
Virginia Beach, VA 23451-2061